KU-505-836

Software Testing

An ISEB Foundation

Brian Hambling (Editor)

Peter Morgan

Angelina Samaroo

Geoff Thompson

Peter Williams

© 2007 The British Computer Society

The right of Brian Hambling, Peter Morgan, Angelina Samaroo, Geoff Thompson and Peter Williams to be identified as authors of this Work has been asserted by them in accordance with sections 77 and 78 of the Copyright, Designs and Patents Act 1988.

All rights reserved. Apart from any fair dealing for the purposes of research or private study, or criticism or review, as permitted by the Copyright Designs and Patents Act 1988, no part of this publication may be reproduced, stored or transmitted in any form or by any means, except with the prior permission in writing of the Publisher, or in the case of reprographic reproduction, in accordance with the terms of the licences issued by the Copyright Licensing Agency. Enquiries for permission to reproduce material outside those terms should be directed to the Publisher.

The British Computer Society
Publishing and Information Products
First Floor, Block D
North Star House
North Star Avenue
Swindon
SN2 1FA
UK

www.bcs.org

ISBN 1-902505-79-4
ISBN13 978-1-902505-79-4

British Cataloguing in Publication Data.
A CIP catalogue record for this book is available at the British Library.

All trademarks, registered names etc. acknowledged in this publication are to be the property of their respective owners.

Disclaimer:
The views expressed in this book are of the author(s) and do not necessarily reflect the views of the British Computer Society except where explicitly stated as such.
Although every care has been taken by the authors and the British Computer Society in the preparation of the publication, no warranty is given by the authors or the British Computer Society as Publisher as to the accuracy or completeness of the information contained within it and neither the authors nor the British Computer Society shall be responsible or liable for any loss or damage whatsoever arising by virtue of such information or any instructions or advice contained within this publication or by any of the aforementioned.

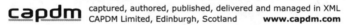

captured, authored, published, delivered and managed in XML
CAPDM Limited, Edinburgh, Scotland   www.capdm.com

Printed and bound in Great Britain by Antony Rowe Ltd, Chippenham, Wiltshire

Software Testing
An ISEB Foundation

Books are to be returned on or before
the last date below.

27/9

LIBREX-

WITHDRAWN

LIVERPOOL JMU LIBRARY

3 1111 01212 1974

The British Computer Society

BCS is the leading professional body for the IT industry. With members in over 100 countries, BCS is the professional and learned Society in the field of computers and information systems.

BCS is responsible for setting standards for the IT profession. It is also leading the change in public perception and appreciation of the economic and social importance of professionally managed IT projects and programmes. In this capacity, the Society advises, informs and persuades industry and government on successful IT implementation.

IT is affecting every part of our lives and that is why BCS is determined to promote IT as the profession of the 21st century.

Joining BCS

BCS qualifications, products and services are designed with your career plans in mind. We not only provide essential recognition through professional qualifications but also offer many other useful benefits to our members at every level.

BCS membership demonstrates your commitment to professional development. It helps to set you apart from other IT practitioners and provides industry recognition of your skills and experience. Employers and customers increasingly require proof of professional qualifications and competence. Professional membership confirms your competence and integrity and sets an independent standard that people can trust. Professional Membership (MBCS) is the pathway to Chartered IT Professional (CITP) Status.

www.bcs.org/membership

Further Information

Further information about BCS can be obtained from: The British Computer Society, First Floor, Block D, North Star House, North Star Avenue, Swindon, SN2 1FA, UK.

Telephone: 0845 300 4417 (UK only) or + 44 (0)1793 417 424 (overseas)

Email: customerservice@hq.bcs.org.uk

Web: www.bcs.org

Contents

List of Figures and Tables

Abbreviations

AUT   Application Under Test

BACS   Banks Automated Clearing Service

CASE   Computer-Aided Software Engineering

CMMi   Capability Maturity Model Integration

DLL   Dynamically Linked Library

FTP   Fundamental Test Process

GUI   Graphical User Interface

ISEB   Information Systems Examination Board

ISTQB   International Software Testing Qualifications Board

MISRA   Motor Industry Software Reliability Association

RAD   Rapid Application Development

RUP   Rational Unified Process

SDLC   Software Development Life Cycle

SIGiST   Special Interest Group in Software Testing

SQL   Structured Query Language

STT   State Transition Table

TPI   Test Process Improvement

UML   Unified Modeling Language

XML   Extensible Markup Language

Contributors

Brian Hambling has experienced software development from a developer's, project manager's and quality manager's perspective in a career spanning over 30 years. He has worked in areas as diverse as real-time avionics, legacy systems maintenance and e-business strategies. He contributed to the development of software quality standards while at the Ministry of Defence and later became the head of systems and software engineering at Thames Polytechnic (now the University of Greenwich). He was general manager of Microgen IQA (formerly ImagoQA), a specialist company providing consultancy in software testing and quality assurance primarily to the financial services sector. He is currently involved in the international roll-out of the ISEB software testing exams.

Peter Morgan is a freelance testing practitioner. He has been working as a hands-on tester for a number of years, often on projects with over 30 testers. He has worked for organizations including Fujitsu Services, Nationwide Building Society, Hutchison 3G and BT Syntegra. He is a member of the ISEB software testing accreditation and examination panels, and has presented papers at several testing conferences, including EuroSTAR. He has a degree from the London School of Economics and is an active member of BCS and especially its Special Interest Group in Software Testing (SIGiST).

Angelina Samaroo began her career in the defence sector, where she worked on the Tornado ADV. In 1995 she was awarded Chartered Engineer status by the Royal Aeronautical Society. Early in her career she took an interest in developing staff, managing the training of new engineers across the company, to the standards laid down by the IEE (now the IET). She is an instructor for the ISEB Foundation and Practitioner Courses in Software Testing. She has also instructed delegates in other aspects of testing, such as unit testing, user acceptance testing and managing testing projects, in the UK, Europe, North America and Australia.

Geoff Thompson has been involved in testing for nearly 20 years, specializing in test process and test strategy, test management and process improvement. He is currently services director for the consulting organization Experimentus Ltd. He is a founder member of the ISEB Software Testing Qualification Board and was directly involved in the creation of, and is the UK representative on, the ISTQB. He is also the vice-chairman of the BCS SIGiST Committee. He was awarded the UK Test Manager of the Year Award in 2004.

Peter Williams previously worked in methods and systems improvement before moving into systems development and subsequently software testing. He has been a self-employed contract test manager or consultant in both financial services and the public sector. He has evaluated test processes and subsequently implemented improvements, at various organizations, including test management and execution tools as appropriate. He has an MSc in computing from the Open University and is chairman of the Examinations Panel for the ISEB Foundation Certificate in Software Testing.

Introduction

NATURE AND PURPOSE OF THE BOOK

The Information Systems Examination Board (ISEB) of the British Computer Society (www.bcs.org.uk/iseb) instigated the Foundation Certificate in Software Testing in 1998; since then over 20,000 Foundation Certificates have been awarded. The more advanced Practitioner Certificate, for which a Foundation Certificate is a prerequisite, was initiated in 2002 and, at the time of writing (Spring 2006) just under 1,000 of these certificates have been awarded.

In 2001 the International Software Testing Qualifications Board (ISTQB) (www.istqb.org) was set up, to offer a similar certification scheme to as many countries as wished to join this international testing community. The UK was a founding member of ISTQB and, in 2005, adopted the ISTQB Foundation Certificate Syllabus as the basis of examinations for the Foundation Certificate in the UK.

This book has been written specifically to help potential candidates for the ISEB/ISTQB Foundation Certificate in Software Testing to prepare for the examination. The book is therefore structured to support learning of the key ideas in the syllabus quickly and efficiently for those who do not plan to attend a course, and to support structured revision for anyone preparing for the exam.

In this introductory chapter we will explain the nature and purpose of the Foundation Certificate and provide an insight into the way the syllabus is structured and the way the book is structured to support learning in the various syllabus areas. Finally we offer guidance on the best way to use this book, either as a learning resource or as a revision resource.

PURPOSE OF FOUNDATION

The Software Testing Foundation Certificate is the first level of a hierarchy of certificates, and it is designed to lead naturally into the next level, known as the Practitioner Certificate. At the time of writing the third level has not yet been defined.

The Foundation Certificate provides a very broad introduction to the whole discipline of software testing. As a result coverage of topics is variable, with some only briefly mentioned and others studied in some detail. The arrangement of the syllabus and the required levels of understanding are explained in the next section.

The authors of the syllabus have aimed it at people with varying levels of experience in testing, including those with no experience at all. This makes the certificate accessible to those who are or who aim to be specialist testers, but also to those who require a more general understanding of testing, such as project managers and software development managers. One specific aim of this certificate is to prepare certificate holders for the next level of certification, but the Foundation Certificate has sufficient breadth and depth of coverage to stand alone.

THE FOUNDATION CERTIFICATE SYLLABUS

Syllabus content and structure

The syllabus is broken down into six main sections, each of which has associated with it a minimum contact time that must be included within any accredited training course:

(1) Fundamentals of testing (155 minutes)
(2) Testing throughout the software life cycle (135 minutes)
(3) Static techniques (60 minutes)
(4) Test design techniques (255 minutes)
(5) Test management (180 minutes)
(6) Tool support for testing (80 minutes)

The relative timings are a reliable guide to the amount of time that should be spent studying each section of the syllabus. These timings are further broken down for each topic within a section.

Each section of the syllabus also includes a list of learning objectives that provides candidates with a guide to what they should know when they have completed their study of a section and a guide to what can be expected to be asked in an examination. The learning objectives can be used to check that learning or revision is adequate for each topic. In the book, which is structured around the syllabus sections, we have presented the learning objectives for each section at the beginning of the relevant chapter, and the summary at the end of each chapter confirms how those learning objectives have been addressed.

Finally, each topic in the syllabus has associated with it a level of understanding, represented by the legend K1, K2 or K3:

- Level of understanding K1 is associated with recall, so that a topic labelled K1 contains information that a candidate should be able to remember but not necessarily use or explain.
- Level of understanding K2 is associated with the ability to explain a topic or to classify information or make comparisons.
- Level of understanding K3 is associated with the ability to apply a topic in a practical setting.

The level of understanding influences the level and type of questions that can be expected to be asked about that topic in the examination. More detail about the question style and about the examination is given in Chapter 7. Example questions, written to the level and in the formats used in the examination, are included within each chapter to provide generous examination practice.

Syllabus map

The syllabus can usefully be viewed as a mind map, as shown in Figure 0.1. In this representation the main sections of the syllabus, corresponding to chapters in the book, provide the first level of ordering. The next level provides the breakdown into topics within each section. In most cases the syllabus breaks topics down even further, but the level of breakdown is omitted from the diagram for clarity. Figure 0.1 enables the entire syllabus to be viewed and is potentially useful as a tracking mechanism to identify visually which parts of the syllabus need most attention and which parts you feel are well understood. By recognizing the relative strengths and weaknesses by topic within sections it is easier to understand the nature and extent of the weakness. For example, problems with certain black-box techniques that are not also associated with white-box techniques and experience-based techniques should give confidence in the overall section on test case design techniques. It is also possible to identify how many marks are 'at risk' from this weakness so that you can plan where to spend most revision time and, perhaps, decide which weaknesses you feel able to leave until after the examination.

RELATIONSHIP OF THE BOOK TO THE SYLLABUS

The book is structured into chapters that mirror the sections of the syllabus so that you can work your way through the whole syllabus or select topics that are of particular interest or concern. The structure enables you to go straight to the place you need, with confidence either that what you need to know will be covered there and nowhere else, or that relevant cross references will be provided.

Each chapter of the book incorporates the learning objectives from the syllabus and identifies the required level of understanding for each topic. Each chapter also includes examples of typical examination questions to enable you to assess your current knowledge of a topic before you read the chapter, and further questions at the end of each chapter to provide practice in answering typical examination questions. Topics requiring K3 level of understanding are presented with worked examples as a model for the level of application expected from real examination questions. Answers are provided for all questions, and the rationale for the correct answer is discussed for all practice questions.

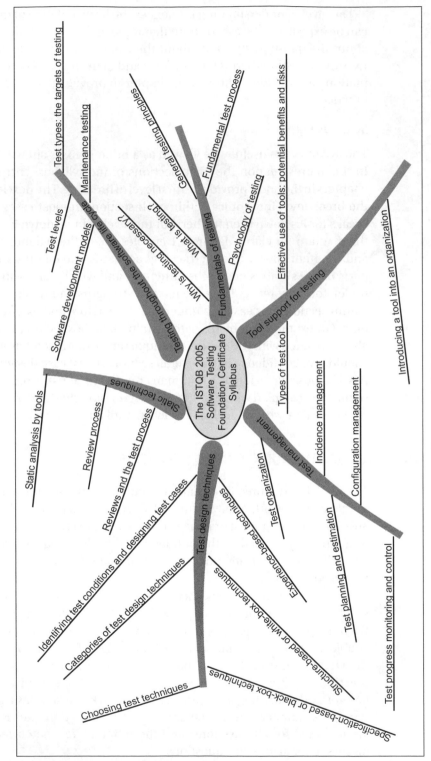

FIGURE 0.1 *Syllabus map*

A final chapter explains the Foundation Certificate examination strategy and provides guidance on how to prepare for the examination and how to manage the examination experience to maximize your own performance.

HOW TO GET THE BEST OUT OF THIS BOOK

This book is designed for use by different groups of people. If you are using the book as an alternative to attending an accredited course you will probably find the first method of using the book described below to be of greatest value. If you are using the book as a revision aid you may find the second approach more appropriate. In either case you would be well advised to acquire a copy of the syllabus (available from www.istqb.org) and a copy of the sample examination paper (available from ISEB) as reference documents, though neither is essential and the book stands alone as a learning and revision aid.

Using the book as a learning aid

For those of you using the book as an alternative to attending an accredited course the first step is to familiarize yourself with the syllabus structure and content by skim reading the opening sections of each chapter where the learning objectives are identified for each topic. You may then find it helpful to turn to Chapter 7 and become familiar with the structure of the examination and the types and levels of questions that you can expect in the examination. From here you can then work through each of the six main chapters in any sequence before returning to Chapter 7 to remind yourself of the main elements of the examination.

For each chapter begin by attempting the self-assessment questions at the beginning to get initial confirmation of your level of confidence in the topics covered by that chapter. This may help you to prioritize how you spend your time. Work first through the chapters where your knowledge is weakest, attempting all the exercises and following through all the worked examples. Read carefully through the chapters where your knowledge is less weak but still not good enough to pass the exam. You can be more selective with exercises and examples here, but make sure you attempt the practice questions at the end of the chapters. For the areas where you feel strong you can use the chapter for revision, but remember to attempt the practice questions to confirm positively your initial assessment of your level of knowledge. Every chapter contains a summary section that reiterates the learning objectives, so reading the first and last sections of a chapter will help you to understand how your current level of knowledge relates to the level required to pass the examination. The best confirmation of this is to attempt questions at the appropriate K level for each topic; these are provided in the book.

Using the book as a revision aid

If you are using this book for final revision, perhaps after completing an accredited course, you might like to begin by using a selection of the example questions at the end of each chapter as a 'mock examination'. The inform-ation in Chapter 7 will enable you to construct a properly balanced mock exam of your own. Your mock exam will provide some experience of answer-ing typical questions under the same time pressures that you will experience in the real examination, and this will provide you with a fairly reliable guide to your current state of readiness to take the real examination. You can also discover which areas most need revision from your performance in the mock exam, and this will guide you as you plan your revision.

Revise first where you feel weakest. You can use the opening sections of each chapter, containing the learning objectives and the self-assessment questions, together with the summary at the end of each chapter to refine further your awareness of your own weaknesses. From here you can target your studies very accurately. Remember that every K3 topic will have at least one worked example and some exercises to help you build your confidence before tackling questions at the level set in the real examination.

You can get final confirmation of your readiness to take the real examina-tion by taking the sample examination paper provided by ISEB.

1 The Fundamentals of Testing

PETER MORGAN

BACKGROUND

If you were buying a new car, you would not expect to take delivery from the showroom with a scratch down the side of the vehicle. The car should have five wheels, a steering wheel, an engine and all the other essential components, and it should come with appropriate documentation, with all pre-sales checks completed and passed satisfactorily. The car you receive should be the car described in the sales literature; it should have the correct engine size, the correct colour scheme, and whatever extras you have ordered, and performance in areas such as fuel consumption and maximum speed should match published figures. In short, a level of expectation is set by brochures, by your experience of sitting in the driving seat, and probably by a test drive. If your expectations are not met you will feel justifiably aggrieved.

This kind of expectation seems not to apply to new software installations; examples of software being delivered not working as expected, or not working at all, are common. Why is this? There is no single cause that can be rectified to solve the problem, but one important contributing factor is the inadequacy of the testing to which software applications are exposed.

Software testing is neither complex nor difficult to implement, yet it is a discipline that is seldom applied with anything approaching the necessary rigour to provide confidence in delivered software. Software testing is costly in human effort or in the technology that can multiply the effect of human effort, yet is seldom implemented at a level that will provide any assurance that software will operate effectively, efficiently or even correctly.

This book explores the fundamentals of this important but neglected discipline to provide a basis on which a practical and cost-effective software testing regime can be constructed.

INTRODUCTION

In this opening chapter we have three very important objectives to achieve. First, we will introduce you to the fundamental ideas that underpin the discipline of software testing, and this will involve the use and explanation of some new terminology. Secondly, we will establish the structure that we have used throughout the book to help you to use the book as a learning and revision aid. Thirdly, we will use this chapter to point forward to the content of later chapters.

We begin by defining what we expect you to get from reading this chapter. The learning objectives below are based on those defined in the Software

Foundation Certificate syllabus (ISTQB, 2005), so you need to ensure that you have achieved all of these objectives before attempting the examination.

Learning objectives

The learning objectives for this chapter are listed below. You can confirm that you have achieved these by using the self-assessment questions at the start of the chapter, the 'Check of understanding' boxes distributed throughout the text, and the example examination questions provided at the end of the chapter. The chapter summary will remind you of the key ideas.

The sections are allocated a K number to represent the level of understanding required for that section; where an individual topic has a lower K number than the section as a whole, this is indicated for that topic; for an explanation of the K numbers see the Introduction.

Why is testing necessary? (K2)

- Describe, with examples, the way in which a defect in software can cause harm to a person, to the environment or to a company.
- Distinguish between the root cause of a defect and its effects.
- Give reasons why testing is necessary by giving examples.
- Describe why testing is part of quality assurance and give examples of how testing contributes to higher quality.
- Recall the terms mistake, defect, failure and the corresponding terms error and bug. (K1)

What is testing? (K2)

- Recall the common objectives of testing. (K1)
- Describe the purpose of testing in software development, maintenance and operations as a means to find defects, provide confidence and information, and prevent defects.

General testing principles (K2)

- Explain the fundamental principles in testing.

Fundamental test process (K1)

- Recall the fundamental test activities from planning to test closure activities and the main tasks of each test activity.

The psychology of testing (K2)

- Recall that the success of testing is influenced by psychological factors (K1):
  - ✦ clear objectives;
  - ✦ a balance of self-testing and independent testing;
  - ✦ recognition of courteous communication and feedback on defects.
- Contrast the mindset of a tester and of a developer.

Self-assessment questions

The following questions have been designed to enable you to check your current level of understanding for the topics in this chapter. The answers are given at the end of the chapter.

Question SA1 (K1)

A bug or defect is:

a.   a mistake made by a person;
b.   a run-time problem experienced by a user;
c.   the result of an error or mistake;
d.   the result of a failure, which may lead to an error?

Question SA2 (K1)

The effect of testing is to:

a.   increase software quality;
b.   give an indication of the software quality;
c.   enable those responsible for software failures to be identified;
d.   show there are no problems remaining?

Question SA3 (K1)

What is confirmation testing?

a.   running the same test again in the same circumstances to reproduce the problem;
b.   a cursory run through a test pack to see if any new errors have been introduced;
c.   checking that the predetermined exit criteria for the test phase have been met;
d.   running a previously failed test against new software/data/documents to see if the problem is solved.

WHY SOFTWARE FAILS

Examples of software failure are depressingly common. Here are some you may recognize:

- The first launch of the European Space Agency Ariane 5 rocket in June 1996 failed after 37½ seconds. A software error caused the rocket to deviate from its vertical ascent, and the self-destruct capabilities were enacted before the then unpredictable flight path resulted in a bigger problem.
- When the UK Government introduced online filing of tax returns, a user could sometimes see the amount that a previous user earned. This was regardless of the physical location of the two applicants.

- In November 2005, information on the UK's top 10 wanted criminals was displayed on a website. The publication of this information was described in newspapers and on morning radio and television and, as a result, many people attempted to access the site. The performance of the website proved inadequate under this load and the website had to be taken offline. The publicity created performance peaks beyond the capacity of the website.

- When a well-known online book retailer first went live, ordering a negative number of books meant that the transaction sum involved was refunded to the 'purchaser'. Development staff had not anticipated that anyone would attempt to purchase a negative number of books. Code was developed to allow refunds to customers to be made by administrative staff – but self-requested refunds are not valid.

- A small, one-line, change in the billing system of an electrical provider blacked out the whole of a major US city.

What is it about these examples that make them so startling? Is it a sense that something fairly obvious was missed? Is it the feeling that, expensive and important as they were, the systems were allowed to enter service before they were ready? Do you think these systems were adequately tested? Obviously they were not, but in this book we want to explore why this was the case and why these kinds of failure continue to plague us.

To understand what is going on we need to start at the beginning, with the people who design systems. Do they make mistakes? Of course they do. People make mistakes because they are fallible, but there are also many pressures that make mistakes more likely. Pressures such as deadlines, complexity of systems and organizations, and changing technology all bear down on designers of systems and increase the likelihood of errors in specifications, in designs and in software code. These errors are where major system failures usually begin. If a document with an error in it is used to specify a component the component will be faulty and will probably exhibit incorrect behaviour. If this faulty component is built into a system the system may fail. While failure is not always guaranteed, it is likely that errors in specifications will lead to faulty components and faulty components will cause system failure.

An error (or mistake) leads to a defect, which can cause an observed failure (Figure 1.1).

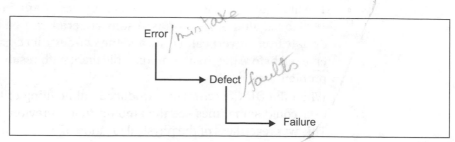

FIGURE 1.1   *Effect of an error*

There are other reasons why systems fail. Environmental conditions such as the presence of radiation, magnetism, electronic fields or pollution can affect the operation of hardware and firmware and lead to system failure.

If we want to avoid failure we must either avoid errors and faults or find them and rectify them. Testing can contribute to both avoidance and rectification, as we will see when we have looked at the testing process in a little more detail. One thing is clear: if we wish to influence errors with testing we need to begin testing as soon as we begin making errors – right at the beginning of the development process – and we need to continue testing until we are confident that there will be no serious system failures – right at the end of the development process.

Before we move on, let us just remind ourselves of the importance of what we are considering. Incorrect software can harm:

- people (e.g. by causing an aircraft crash in which people die, or by causing a hospital life support system to fail);
- companies (e.g. by causing incorrect billing, which results in the company losing money);
- the environment (e.g. by releasing chemicals or radiation into the atmosphere).

Software failures can sometimes cause all three of these at once. The scenario of a train carrying nuclear waste being involved in a crash has been explored to help build public confidence in the safety of transporting nuclear waste by train. A failure of the train's on-board systems or of the signalling system that controls the train's movements could lead to catastrophic results. This may not be likely (we hope it is not) but it is a possibility that could be linked with software failure. Software failures, then, can lead to:

- Loss of money
- Loss of time
- Loss of business reputation
- Injury
- Death

KEEPING SOFTWARE UNDER CONTROL

With all of the examples we have seen so far, what common themes can we identify? There may be several themes that we could draw out of the examples, but one theme is clear: either insufficient testing or the wrong type of testing was done. More and better software testing seems a reasonable aim, but that aim is not quite as simple to achieve as we might expect.

Exhaustive testing of complex systems is not possible

With the Ariane 5 rocket launch, a particular software module was reused from the Ariane 4 programme. Only part of the functionality of the module was required, but the module was incorporated without changes. The unused functionality of the reused module indirectly caused a directional nozzle to move in an uncontrolled way because certain variables were incorrectly updated. In an Ariane 4 rocket the module would have performed as required, but in the Ariane 5 environment this malfunction in an area of software not even in use caused a catastrophic failure. The failure is well documented, but what is clear is that conditions were encountered in the first few seconds after the launch that were not expected, and therefore had not been tested.

If every possible test had been run, the problem would have been detected. However, if every test had been run, the testing would still be running now, and the ill-fated launch would never have taken place; this illustrates one of the general principles of software testing, which are explained below. With large and complex systems it will never be possible to test everything exhaustively; in fact it is impossible to test even moderately complex systems exhaustively.

In the Ariane 5 case it would be unhelpful to say that not enough testing was done; for this particular project, and for many others of similar complexity, that would certainly always be the case. In the Ariane 5 case the problem was that the right sort of testing was not done because the problem had not been detected.

Testing and risk

Risk is inherent in all software development. The system may not work or the project to build it may not be completed on time, for example. These uncertainties become more significant as the system complexity and the implications of failure increase. Intuitively, we would expect to test an automatic flight control system more than we would test a video game system. Why? Because the risk is greater. There is a greater probability of failure in the more complex system and the impact of failure is also greater. What we test, and how much we test it, must be related in some way to the risk. Greater risk implies more and better testing.

There is much more on risk and risk management in Chapter 5.

Testing and quality

Quality is notoriously hard to define. If a system meets its users' requirements that constitutes a good starting point. In the examples we looked at earlier the online tax returns system had an obvious functional weakness in allowing one user to view another user's details. While the user community for such a system is potentially large and disparate, it is hard to imagine any user that would find that situation anything other than unacceptable. In the top 10 criminals example the problem was slightly different. There was no failure of functionality in this case; the system was simply swamped by requests for access. This is an example of a non-functional failure, in that the system was not able to deliver its services to its users because it was not designed to handle the peak load that materialized after radio and TV coverage.

Of course the software development process, like any other, must balance competing demands for resources. If we need to deliver a system faster (i.e. in less time), for example, it will usually cost more. The items at the vertices of the triangle of resources in Figure 1.2 are time, money and quality. These three affect one another, and also influence the features that are or are not included in the delivered softwares.

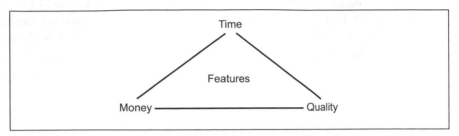

FIGURE 1.2 *Resources triangle*

One role for testing is to ensure that key functional and non-functional requirements are examined before the system enters service and any defects are reported to the development team for rectification. Testing cannot directly remove defects, nor can it directly enhance quality. By reporting defects it makes their removal possible and so contributes to the enhanced quality of the system. In addition, the systematic coverage of a software product in testing allows at least some aspects of the quality of the software to be measured. Testing is one component in the overall quality assurance activity that seeks to ensure that systems enter service without defects that can lead to serious failures.

Deciding when 'enough is enough'

How much testing is enough, and how do we decide when to stop testing?

We have so far decided that we cannot test everything, even if we would wish to. We also know that every system is subject to risk of one kind or another and that there is a level of quality that is acceptable for a given system. These are the factors we will use to decide how much testing to do.

The most important aspect of achieving an acceptable result from a finite and limited amount of testing is prioritization. Do the most important tests first so that at any time you can be certain that the tests that have been done are more important than the ones still to be done. Even if the testing activity is cut in half it will still be true that the most important testing has been done. The most important tests will be those that test the most important aspects of the system: they will test the most important functions as defined by the users or sponsors of the system, and the most important non-functional behaviour, and they will address the most significant risks.

The next most important aspect is setting criteria that will give you an objective test of whether it is safe to stop testing, so that time and all the other pressures do not confuse the outcome. These criteria, usually known as completion criteria, set the standards for the testing activity by defining areas such as how much of the software is to be tested (this is covered in more detail in Chapter 4) and what levels of defects can be tolerated in a delivered product (which is covered in more detail in Chapter 5)).

Priorities and completion criteria provide a basis for planning (which will be covered in Chapter 2 and Chapter 5) but the triangle of resources in Figure 1.2 still applies. In the end, the desired level of quality and risk may have to be compromised, but our approach ensures that we can still determine how much testing is required to achieve the agreed levels and we can still be certain that any reduction in the time or effort available for testing will not affect the balance – the most important tests will still be those that have already been done whenever we stop.

CHECK OF UNDERSTANDING

(1) Describe the interaction between errors, defects and failures.

(2) Software failures can cause losses. Give three consequences of software failures.

(3) What are the vertices of the 'triangle of resources'?

WHAT TESTING IS AND WHAT TESTING DOES

So far we have worked with an intuitive idea of what testing is. We have recognized that it is an activity used to reduce risk and improve quality by finding defects, which is all true. However, we need to understand a little more about how software testing works in practice before we can think about how to implement effective testing.

Testing and debugging

Testing and debugging are different kinds of activity, both of which are very important. Debugging is the process that developers go through to identify the cause of bugs or defects in code and undertake corrections. Ideally some check of the correction is made, but this may not extend to checking that other areas of the system have not been inadvertently affected by the correction. Testing, on the other hand, is a systematic exploration of a component or system with the main aim of finding and reporting defects. Testing does not include correction of defects – these are passed on to the developer to correct. Testing does, however, ensure that changes and corrections are checked for their effect on other parts of the component or system.

Effective debugging is essential before testing begins to raise the level of quality of the component or system to a level that is worth testing, i.e. a level that is sufficiently robust to enable rigorous testing to be performed. Debugging does not give confidence that the component or system meets its requirements completely. Testing makes a rigorous examination of the behaviour of a component or system and reports all defects found for the development team to correct. Testing then repeats enough tests to ensure that defect corrections have been effective. So both are needed to achieve a quality result.

Static testing and dynamic testing

Static testing is the term used for testing where the code is not exercised. This may sound strange, but remember that failures often begin with a human error, namely a mistake in a document such as a specification. We need to test these because errors are much cheaper to fix than defects or failures (as you will see). That is why testing should start as early as possible, another basic principle explained in more detail later in this chapter. Static testing involves techniques such as reviews, which can be effective in preventing defects, e.g. by removing ambiguities and errors from specification documents; this is a topic in its own right and is covered in detail in Chapter 3. Dynamic testing is the kind that exercises the program under test with some test data, so we speak of test execution in this context. The discipline of software testing encompasses both static and dynamic testing.

Testing as a process

We have already seen that there is much more to testing than test execution. Before test execution there is some preparatory work to do to design the tests and set them up; after test execution there is some work needed to record the results and check whether the tests are complete. Even more important than this is deciding what we are trying to achieve with the testing and setting clear objectives for each test. A test designed to give confidence that a program functions according to its specification, for example, will be quite different from one designed to find as many defects as possible. We define a test process to ensure that we do not miss critical steps and that we do things in the right order. We will return to this important topic later, where we explain the fundamental test process in detail.

Testing as a set of techniques

The final challenge is to ensure that the testing we do is effective testing. It might seem paradoxical, but a good test is one that finds a defect if there is one present. A test that finds no defect has consumed resources but added no value; a test that finds a defect has created an opportunity to improve the quality of the product. How do we design tests that find defects? We actually do two things to maximize the effectiveness of the tests. First we use well-proven test design techniques, and a selection of the most important of these is explained in detail in Chapter 4. The techniques are all based on certain testing principles that have been discovered and documented over the years, and these principles are the second mechanism we use to ensure that tests are effective. Even when we cannot apply rigorous test design for some reason (such as time pressures) we can still apply the general principles to guide our testing. We turn to these next.

> ## CHECK OF UNDERSTANDING
>
> (1) Describe static testing and dynamic testing.
> (2) What is debugging?
> (3) What other elements apart from 'test execution' are included in 'testing'?

GENERAL TESTING PRINCIPLES

Testing is a very complex activity, and the software problems described earlier highlight that it can be difficult to do well. We now describe some general testing principles that help testers, principles that have been developed over the years from a variety of sources. These are not all obvious, but their purpose is to guide testers, and prevent the types of problems described previously. Testers use these principles with the test techniques described in Chapter 4.

Testing shows the presence of bugs

Running a test through a software system can only show that one or more defects exist. Testing cannot show that the software is error free. Consider whether the top 10 wanted criminals website was error free. There were no functional defects, yet the website failed. In this case the problem was non-functional and the absence of defects was not adequate as a criterion for release of the website into operation.

In Chapter 2, we will discuss confirmation testing, when a previously failed test is rerun, to show that under the same conditions, a previously reported problem no longer exists. In this type of situation, testing can show that one particular problem no longer exists.

Although there may be other objectives, usually the main purpose of testing is to find defects. Therefore tests should be designed to find as many defects as possible.

Exhaustive testing is impossible

If testing finds problems, then surely you would expect more testing to find additional problems, until eventually we would have found them all. We discussed exhaustive testing earlier when looking at the Ariane 5 rocket launch, and concluded that for large complex systems, exhaustive testing is not possible. However, could it be possible to test small pieces of software exhaustively, and only incorporate exhaustively tested code into large systems?

> **Exhaustive testing – a test approach in which all possible data combinations are used. This includes implicit data combinations present in the state of the software/data at the start of testing.**

Consider a small piece of software where one can enter a password that can contain up to three characters, with no consecutive repeating characters. Using only western alphabetic capital letters, there are $26 \times 26 \times 26$ permutations of inputs – a large number. If we have a standard keyboard, there are not $26 \times 26 \times 26$ permutations, but a much higher number, $256 \times 256 \times 256$, or 2^{24}. Even then, the number of possibilities is higher. What happens if three characters are entered, and the 'delete last character' right arrow key removes the last two? Are special key combinations accepted, or do they cause system actions (Ctrl + P, for example)? What about entering a character, and waiting 20 minutes before entering the other two characters? It may be the same combination of keystrokes, but the circumstances are different. We can also include the situation where the 20-minute break occurs over the change-of-day interval. It is not possible to say whether there are any defects until all possible input combinations have been tried.

Even in this small example, there are many, many possible data combinations to attempt.

Unless the application under test (AUT) has an extremely simple logical structure and limited input, it is not possible to test all possible combinations of data input and circumstances. For this reason, risk and priorities are used to concentrate on the most important aspects to test. Both 'risk' and 'priorities' are covered later in more detail. Their use is important to ensure that the most important parts are tested.

Early testing

When discussing why software fails, we briefly mentioned the idea of early testing. This principle is important because, as a proposed deployment date approaches, time pressure can increase dramatically. There is a real danger that testing will be squeezed, and this is bad news if the only testing we are doing is after all the development has been completed. The earlier the testing activity is started, the longer the elapsed time available. Testers do not have to wait until software is available to test.

Work-products are created throughout the software development life cycle (SDLC). As soon as these are ready, we can test them. In Chapter 2, we will see that requirement documents are the basis for acceptance testing, so the creation of acceptance tests can begin as soon as requirement documents are available. As we create these tests, it will highlight the contents of the requirements. Are individual requirements testable? Can we find ambiguous or missing requirements?

Many problems in software systems can be traced back to missing or incorrect requirements. We will look at this in more detail when we discuss reviews in Chapter 3. The use of reviews can break the 'mistake–defect–failure' cycle. In early testing we are trying to find errors and defects before they are passed to the next stage of the development process. Early testing techniques are attempting to show that what is produced as a system specification, for example, accurately reflects that which is in the requirement documents. Ed Kit (Kit, 1995) discusses identifying and eliminating errors at the part of the SDLC in which they are introduced. If an error/defect is introduced in the coding activity, it is preferable to detect and correct it at this stage. If a problem is not corrected at the stage in which it is introduced, this leads to what Kit calls 'errors of migration'. The result is rework. We need to rework not just the part where the mistake was made, but each subsequent part where the error has been replicated. A defect found at acceptance testing where the original mistake was in the requirements will require several work-products to be reworked, and subsequently to be retested.

Studies have been done on the cost impacts of errors at the different development stages. Whilst it is difficult to put figures on the relative costs of finding defects at different levels in the SDLC, Table 1.1 does concentrate the mind!

TABLE 1.1   *Comparative cost to correct errors*

Stage error is found	Comparative cost
Requirements	$1
Coding	$10
Program testing	$100
System testing	$1,000
User acceptance testing	$10,000
Live running	$100,000

This is known as the cost escalation model

What is undoubtedly true is that the graph of the relative cost of early and late identification/correction of defects rises very steeply (Figure 1.3).

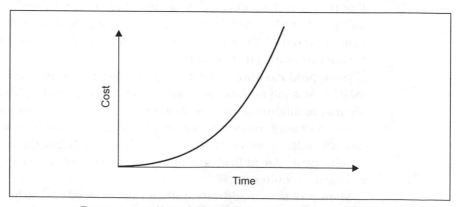

FIGURE 1.3   *Effect of identification time on cost of errors*

The earlier a problem (defect) is found, the less it costs to fix.

The objectives of various stages of testing can be different. For example, in the review processes, we may focus on whether the documents are consistent and no errors have been introduced when the documents were produced. Other stages of testing can have other objectives. The important point is that testing has defined objectives.

Defect clustering

Problems do occur in software! It is a fact. Once testing has identified (most of) the defects in a particular application, it is at first surprising that the spread of defects is not uniform. In a large application, it is often a small number of modules that exhibit the majority of the problems. This can be for a variety of reasons, some of which are:

- System complexity.
- Volatile code.
- The effects of change upon change.
- Development staff experience.
- Development staff inexperience.

This is the application of the Pareto principle to software testing: approximately 80 per cent of the problems are found in about 20 per cent of the modules. It is useful if testing activity reflects this spread of defects, and targets areas of the application under test where a high proportion of defects can be found. However, it must be remembered that testing should not concentrate exclusively on these parts. There may be fewer defects in the remaining code, but testers still need to search diligently for them.

The pesticide paradox

Running the same set of tests continually will not continue to find new defects. Developers will soon know that the test team always tests the boundaries of conditions, for example, so they will test these conditions before the software is delivered. This does not make defects elsewhere in the code less likely, so continuing to use the same test set will result in decreasing effectiveness of the tests. Using other techniques will find different defects.

For example, a small change to software could be specifically tested and an additional set of tests performed, aimed at showing that no additional problems have been introduced (this is known as regression testing). However, the software may fail in production because the regression tests are no longer relevant to the requirements of the system or the test objectives. Any regression test set needs to change to reflect business needs, and what are now seen as the most important risks. Regression testing will be discussed later in this chapter, but is covered in more detail in Chapter 2.

Testing is context dependent

Different testing is necessary in different circumstances. A website where information can merely be viewed will be tested in a different way to an e-commerce site, where goods can be bought using credit/debit cards. We need to test an air traffic control system with more rigour than an application for calculating the length of a mortgage.

Risk can be a large factor in determining the type of testing that is needed. The higher the possibility of losses, the more we need to invest in testing the software before it is implemented. A fuller discussion of risk is given in Chapter 5.

For an e-commerce site, we should concentrate on security aspects. Is it possible to bypass the use of passwords? Can 'payment' be made with an invalid credit card, by entering excessive data into the card number? Security testing is an example of a specialist area, not appropriate for all applications. Such types of testing may require specialist staff and software tools. Test tools are covered in more detail in Chapter 6.

Absence of errors fallacy

Software with no known errors is not necessarily ready to be shipped. Does the application under test match up to the users' expectations of it? The fact that no defects are outstanding is not a good reason to ship the software.

Before dynamic testing has begun, there are no defects reported against the code delivered. Does this mean that software that has not been tested (but has no outstanding defects against it) can be shipped? We think not!

> **CHECK OF UNDERSTANDING**
>
> (1) Why is 'zero defects' an insufficient guide to software quality?
> (2) Give three reasons why defect clustering may exist.
> (3) Briefly justify the idea of early testing.

FUNDAMENTAL TEST PROCESS

We previously determined that testing is a process, discussed above. This process is detailed in what has become known as the fundamental test process, a key element of what testers do, and is applicable at all stages of testing.

The most visible part of testing is running one or more tests: test execution. We also have to prepare for running tests, analyse the tests that have been run, and see whether testing is complete. Both planning and analysing are very necessary activities that enhance and amplify the benefits of the test execution itself. It is no good testing without deciding how, when and what to test. Planning is also required for the less formal test approaches such as exploratory testing, covered in more detail in Chapter 4.

The fundamental test process consists of five parts that encompass all aspects of testing (Figure 1.4):

(1) Planning and control.
(2) Analysis and design.
(3) Implementation and execution.
(4) Evaluating exit criteria and reporting.
(5) Test closure activities.

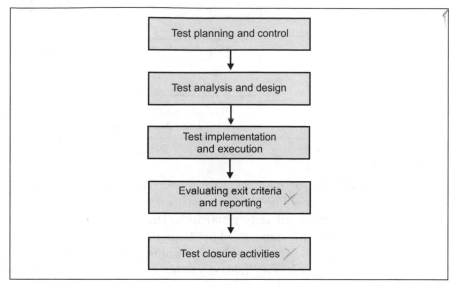

FIGURE 1.4 *Fundamental test process*

Although the main activities are in a broad sequence, they are not undertaken in a rigid way. An earlier activity may need to be revisited. A defect found in test execution can sometimes be resolved by adding functionality that was originally not present (either missing in error, or the new facilities are needed to make the other part correct). The new features themselves have to be tested, so even though implementation and execution are in progress, the 'earlier' activity of analysis and design has to be performed for the new features (Figure 1.5).

We sometimes need to do two or more of the main activities in parallel. Time pressure can mean that we begin test execution before all tests have been designed.

Test planning and control

Planning is determining what is going to be tested, and how this will be achieved. It is where we draw a map; how activities will be done; and who will do them. Test planning is also where we define the test completion criteria. Completion criteria are how we know when testing is finished. Control, on the other hand, is what we do when the activities do not match up with the plans. It is the on-going activity where we compare the progress against the

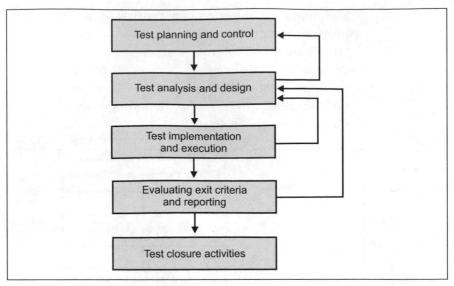

FIGURE 1.5   *Iteration of activities*

plan. As progress takes place, we may need to adjust plans to meet the targets, if this is possible. Therefore we need to undertake both planning and control throughout the testing activities. The activities of planning and control are developed in more detail in Chapter 5.

The main activities of test planning are given below:

- Defining the scope and objectives of testing and identifying risks.
- Determining the test approach (techniques, test items, coverage, identifying and interfacing the teams involved in testing, testware).
- Detailing what is required to do the testing (e.g. people, test environment, PCs).
- Implementing the test policy and/or the test strategy.
- Scheduling the test analysis and design tasks.
- Scheduling test implementation, execution and evaluation.
- Detailing when testing will stop, the exit criteria.

We would normally consider the following parts for test control:

- Measuring and analysing results.
- Comparing expected and actual progress, test coverage and exit criteria.
- Making corrections if things go wrong, and deciding actions.

Test analysis and design

Analysis and design are concerned with the fine detail of what to test (test conditions), and how to combine test conditions into test cases, so that a small number of test cases can cover as many of the test conditions as possible. The analysis and design stage is the bridge between planning and test execution. It is looking backward to the planning (schedules, people, what is going to be tested) and forward to the execution activity (test expected results, what environment will be needed).

Test design involves predicting how the software under test should behave in a given set of circumstances. Sometimes the expected outcome of a test is trivial: when ordering books from an online book retailer, for instance, under no circumstances should money be refunded to the customer's card without intervention from a supervisor. If we do not detail expected outcomes before starting test execution, there is a real danger that we will miss the one item of detail that is vital, but wrong.

These topics will be discussed in more detail in Chapter 4, when test case design techniques are presented. The main points of this activity are as follows:

- Reviewing requirements, architecture, design, interfaces and other parts, which collectively comprise the test basis.
- Analysing test items, the specification, behaviour and structure to identify test conditions and test data required.
- Designing the tests.
- Determining whether the requirements and the system are testable.
- Detailing what the test environment should look like, and whether there are any infrastructure and tools required.

Test implementation and execution

The test implementation and execution activity involves running tests, and this will include where necessary any set-up/tear-down activities for the testing. It will also involve checking the test environment before testing begins. Test execution is the most visible part of testing, but it is not possible without other parts of the fundamental test process. It is not just about running tests. As we have already mentioned, the most important tests need to be run first. How do we know what are the most important tests to run? This is determined during the planning stages, and refined as part of test design.

As tests are run, their outcome needs to be logged, and a comparison made between expected results and actual results. Whenever there is a discrepancy between the expected and actual results, this needs to be investigated. If necessary a test incident should be raised. Each incident requires investigation, although corrective action will not be necessary in every case. Test incidents will be discussed in Chapter 5.

When anything changes (software, data, installation procedures, user documentation, etc.), we need to do two kinds of testing on the software. First of all, tests should be run to make sure that the problem has been fixed. We also need to make sure that the changes have not broken the software elsewhere. These two types are usually called confirmation testing and regression testing, respectively. In confirmation testing we are looking in fine detail at the changed area of functionality, whereas regression testing should cover all the main functions to ensure that no unintended changes have occurred. On a financial system, we should include end of day/end of month/end of year processing, for example, in a regression test pack.

Test implementation and execution is where the most visible test activities are undertaken, and usually have the following parts:

- Developing and prioritizing test cases, creating test data, writing test procedures and, optionally, preparing test harnesses and writing automated test scripts.
- Collecting test cases into test suites, where tests can be run one after another for efficiency.
- Checking the test environment set-up is correct.
- Running test cases in the determined order. This can be manually or using test execution tools.
- Keeping a log of testing activities, including the outcome (pass/fail) and the versions of software, data, tools and testware (scripts, etc.).
- Comparing actual results with expected results.
- Reporting discrepancies as incidents with as much information as possible, including if possible causal analysis (code defect, incorrect test specification, test data error or test execution error).
- Where necessary, repeating test activities when changes have been made following incidents raised. This includes re-execution of a test that previously failed in order to confirm a fix (confirmation testing), execution of a corrected test and execution of previously passed tests to check that defects have not been introduced (regression testing).

Evaluating exit criteria and reporting

Remember that exit criteria were defined during test planning and before test execution started. At the end of test execution, the test manager checks to see if these have been met. If the criteria were that there would be 85 per cent statement coverage (i.e. 85 per cent of all executable statements have been executed (see Chapter 4 for more detail)), and as a result of execution the figure is 75 per cent, there are two possible actions: change the exit criteria, or run more tests. It is possible that even if the preset criteria were met, more tests would be required. Also, writing a test summary for stakeholders would say what was planned, what was achieved, highlight any differences and in particular things that were not tested.

The fourth stage of the fundamental test process, evaluating exit criteria, comprises the following:

- Checking whether the previously determined exit criteria have been met.
- Determining if more tests are needed or if the specified exit criteria need amending.
- Writing up the result of the testing activities for the business sponsors and other stakeholders.

More detail is given on this subject in Chapter 5.

Test closure activities

Testing at this stage has finished. Test closure activities concentrate on making sure that everything is tidied away, reports written, defects closed, and those defects deferred for another phase clearly seen to be as such.

At the end of testing, the test closure stage is composed of the following:

- Ensuring that the documentation is in order; what has been delivered is defined (it may be more or less than originally planned), closing incidents and raising changes for future deliveries, documenting that the system has been accepted.

- Closing down and archiving the test environment, test infrastructure and testware used.

- Passing over testware to the maintenance team.

- Writing down the lessons learned from this testing project for the future, and incorporating lessons to improve the testing process ('testing maturity').

The detail of the test closure activities is discussed in Chapter 5.

CHECK OF UNDERSTANDING

(1) What are the stages in the fundamental test process (in the correct sequence)?

(2) Briefly compare regression testing and confirmation testing.

(3) When should the expected outcome of a test be defined?

THE PSYCHOLOGY OF TESTING

One last topic that we need to address before we move on to the more detailed coverage of topics in the following chapters is the basic psychology behind testing.

A variety of different people may be involved in the total testing effort, and they may be drawn from a broad set of backgrounds. Some will be developers, some professional testers, and some will be specialists, such as those with performance testing skills, whilst others may be users drafted in to assist with acceptance testing. Whoever is involved in testing needs at least some understanding of the skills and techniques of testing to make an effective contribution to the overall testing effort.

Testing can be more effective if it is not undertaken by the individual(s) who wrote the code, for the simple reason that the creator of anything (whether it is software or a work of art) has a special relationship with the created object. The nature of that relationship is such that flaws in the created object are rendered invisible to the creator. For that reason it is important that someone other than the creator should test the object. Of course we do want the developer who builds a component or system to debug it, and even to attempt to test it, but we accept that testing done by that individual cannot be assumed to be complete. Developers can test their own code, but it requires a mindset change, from that of a developer (to prove it works) to that of a tester (trying to show that it does not work). If there are separate individuals involved, there are no potential conflicts of interest. We therefore aim to have the software tested by someone who was not involved in the creation of the software; this approach is called test independence. Below are people who could test software, listed in order of increasing independence:

- Those who wrote the code.
- Members of the same development team.
- Members of a different group (independent test team).
- Members of a different company (a testing consultancy/outsourced).

Of course independence comes at a price; it is much more expensive to use a testing consultancy than to test a program oneself.

Testers and developers think in different ways. However, although we know that testers should be involved from the beginning, it is not always good to get testers involved in code execution at an early stage; there are advantages and disadvantages. Getting developers to test their own code has advantages (as soon as problems are discovered, they can be fixed, without the need for extensive error logs), but also difficulties (it is hard to find your own mistakes). People and projects have objectives, and we all modify actions to blend in with the goals. If a developer has a goal of producing acceptable software by certain dates, then any testing is aimed towards that goal.

If a defect is found in software, the software author may see this as criticism. Testers need to use tact and diplomacy when raising defect reports. Defect reports need to be raised against the software, not against the individual who made the mistake. The mistake may be in the code written, or in one of the documents upon which the code is based (requirement documents or system specification). When we raise defects in a constructive way, bad feeling can be avoided.

We all need to focus on good communication, and work on team building. Testers and developers are not opposed, but working together, with the joint target of better quality systems. Communication needs to be objective, and expressed in impersonal ways:

- The aim is to work together rather than be confrontational. Keep the focus on delivering a quality product.
- Results should be presented in a non-personal way. The work-product may be wrong, so say this in a non-personal way.
- Attempt to understand how others feel; it is possible to discuss problems and **still** leave all parties feeling positive.
- At the end of discussions, confirm that you have both understood and been understood. 'So, am I right in saying that your aim was to deliver on Friday by 12:00, even if you knew there were problems?'

As testers and developers, one of our goals is better quality systems delivered in a timely manner. Good communication between testers and the development teams is one way that this goal can be reached.

CHECK OF UNDERSTANDING

(1) When testing software, who has the highest level of independence?

(2) Contrast the advantages and disadvantages of developers testing their own code.

(3) Suggest three ways that confrontation can be avoided.

SUMMARY

In this chapter, we have looked at key ideas that are used in testing, and introduced some terminology. We examined some of the types of software problems that can occur, and why the blanket explanation of 'insufficient testing' is unhelpful. The problems encountered then led through some questions about the nature of testing, why errors and mistakes are made, and how these can be identified and eliminated. Individual examples enabled us to look at what testing can achieve, and the view that testing does not improve software quality, but provides information about that quality.

We have examined both general testing principles and a standard template for testing: the fundamental test process. These are useful and can be effective in identifying the types of problems we considered at the start of the chapter. The chapter finished by examining how developers and testers think, and looked at different levels of test independence.

This chapter is an introduction to testing, and to themes that are developed later in the book. It is a chapter in its own right, but also points to information that will come later. A rereading of this chapter when you have worked through the rest of the book will place all the main topics into context.

REFERENCES

ISTQB (2005) *Certified Tester Foundation Level Syllabus.* International Software Testing Qualifications Board, Erlangen.

Kit, Edward (1995) *Software Testing in the Real World.* Addison-Wesley, Reading, MA.

Example examination questions with answers

E1. K1 question

Which of the following is correct?

Debugging is:

a. Testing/checking whether the software performs correctly.
b. Checking that a previously reported defect has been corrected.
c. Identifying the cause of a defect, repairing the code and checking the fix is correct.
d. Checking that no unintended consequences have occurred as a result of a fix.

E2. K2 question

Which of the following are aids to good communication, and which hinder it?

(i) Try to understand how the other person feels.
(ii) Communicate personal feelings, concentrating upon individuals.
(iii) Confirm the other person has understood what you have said and vice versa.
(iv) Emphasize the common goal of better quality.
(v) Each discussion is a battle to be won.

a. (i), (ii) and (iii) *aid*, (iv) and (v) *hinder*.
b. (iii), (iv) and (v) *aid*, (i) and (ii) *hinder*.
c. (i), (iii) and (iv) *aid*, (ii) and (v) *hinder*.
d. (ii), (iii) and (iv) *aid*, (i) and (v) *hinder*.

E3. K1 question

Which option is part of the 'implementation and execution' area of the fundamental test process?

a. Developing the tests.
b. Comparing actual and expected results.
c. Writing a test summary.
d. Analysing lessons learnt for future releases.

E4. K1 question

The five parts of the fundamental test process have a broad chronological order. Which of the options gives three different parts in the correct order?

a. Implementation and execution, planning and control, analysis and design.
b. Analysis and design, evaluating exit criteria and reporting, test closure activities.
c. Evaluating exit criteria and reporting, implementation and execution, analysis and design.
d. Evaluating exit criteria and reporting, test closure activities, analysis and design.

E5. K2 question

Which pair of definitions is correct?

a.　Regression testing is checking that the reported defect has been fixed; confirmation testing is testing that there are no additional problems in previously tested software.

b.　Regression testing is checking there are no additional problems in previously tested software; confirmation testing enables developers to isolate the problem.

c.　Regression testing involves running all tests that have been run before; confirmation testing runs new tests.

d.　Regression testing is checking that there are no additional problems in previously tested software, confirmation testing is demonstrating that the reported defect has been fixed.

E6. K1 question

Which statement is **most** true?

a.　Different testing is needed depending upon the application.

b.　All software is tested in the same way.

c.　A technique that finds defects will always find defects.

d.　A technique that has found no defects is not useful.

E7. K1 question

When is testing complete?

a.　When time and budget are exhausted.

b.　When there is enough information for sponsors to make an informed decision about release.

c.　When there are no remaining high priority defects outstanding.

d.　When every data combination has been exercised successfully.

E8. K1 question

Which list of levels of tester independence is in the correct order, starting with the **most** independent first?

a.　Tests designed by the author; tests designed by another member of the development team; tests designed by someone from a different company.

b.　Tests designed by someone from a different department within the company; tests designed by the author; tests designed by someone from a different company.

c.　Tests designed by someone from a different company; tests designed by someone from a different department within the company; tests designed by another member of the development team.

d.　Tests designed by someone from a different department within the company; tests designed by someone from a different company; tests designed by the author.

E9. K2 question

The following statements relate to activities that are part of the fundamental test process.

(i) Evaluating the testability of requirements.
(ii) Repeating testing activities after changes.
(iii) Designing the test environment set up.
(iv) Developing and prioritizing test cases.
(v) Verifying the environment is set up correctly.

Which statement below is TRUE?

a. (i) and (ii) are part of analysis and design, (iii), (iv) and (v) are part of test implementation and execution.

b. (i) and (iii) are part of analysis and design, (ii), (iv) and (v) are part of test implementation and execution.

c. (i) and (v) are part of analysis and design, (ii), (iii) and (iv) are part of test implementation and execution.

d. (i) and (iv) are part of analysis and design, (ii), (iii) and (v) are part of test implementation and execution.

Answers to questions in the chapter

SA1. The correct answer is c.

SA2. The correct answer is b.

SA3. The correct answer is d.

Answers to example questions

E1. The correct answer is c.
   a. is a brief definition of testing.
   b. is confirmation testing.
   d. is regression testing.

E2. The correct answer is c.
   If you are unsure why, revisit the section in this chapter on the psychology of testing.

E3. The correct answer is b.
   a. is part of 'Analysis and design'.
   c. is part of 'Evaluating exit criteria and reporting'.
   d. is part of 'Test closure activities'.

E4. The correct answer is b.
   All other answers have at least one stage of the fundamental test process in the wrong sequence.

E5. The correct answer is d.
   Regression testing is testing that nothing has **regressed**. Confirmation testing **confirms** the fix is correct by running the same test after the fix has been made. No other option has both of these as true.

E6. The correct answer is a.
   This is a restatement of the testing principle 'Testing is context dependent'.

E7. The correct answer is b.
   Sometimes time/money does signify the end of testing, but it is really complete when everything that was set out in advance has been achieved.

E8. The correct answer is c.
   This option has someone **nearer** to the written code in each statement. All other options have not got this order.

E9. The correct answer is b.
   All other answers contain an activity identified as analysis and design that is part of implementation and test execution.

2 Life Cycles

ANGELINA SAMAROO

INTRODUCTION

In the previous chapter, we looked at testing as a concept – what it is and why we should do it. In this chapter we will look at testing as part of overall software development. Clearly testing does not take place in isolation; there must be a product first!

We will refer to work-products and products. A work-product is an intermediate deliverable required to create the final product. Work-products can be documentation or code. The code and associated documentation will become the product when the system is declared ready for release. In software development, work-products are generally created in a series of defined stages, from capturing a customer requirement, to creating the system, to delivering the system. These stages are usually shown as steps within a software development life cycle.

In this chapter we will look at two life-cycle models – sequential and iterative. For each one, the testing process will be described, and the objectives at each stage of testing explained.

Finally, we will look at the different types of testing which can take place throughout the development life cycle.

Learning objectives

The learning objectives for each section are as follows. Each section has been categorized as K2 overall, but individual K1 elements are shown where applicable.

Software development models (K2)
- Understanding of the relationship between development, test activities and work-products in the development life cycle, giving examples based on project and product characteristics and context.
- Recognition that software development models must be adapted to the context of project and product characteristics. (K1)
- Recall of reasons for different levels of testing, and characteristics of good testing in any life-cycle model. (K1)

Test levels (K2)
- Be able to compare the different levels of testing, considering for each the:
  + Major objectives.
  + Typical objectives of testing.

+ Typical targets of testing (e.g. functional or structural) and related work-products.
+ People who test.
+ Types of defects and failures to be identified.

Test types (K2)

- Comparison of the four requirement types (functional, non-functional, structural and change-related) by example.
- Recognition that functional and structural tests can occur at any level. (K1)
- Identification and description of non-functional test types based on non-functional requirements.
- Identification and description of test types based on the analysis of a software system's structure or architecture.
- Explanation of the purpose of confirmation and regression testing.

Maintenance testing (K2)

- Recognition of differences between testing existing systems and new systems, considering:
  + Test types
  + Triggers for testing
  + Amount of testing
- Recall of reasons for maintenance testing (K1):
  + Modification
  + Migration
  + Retirement
- Description of the role of regression testing and impact analysis in maintenance testing.

Self-assessment questions

The following questions have been designed to assess the reader's current knowledge of this topic. The answers are provided at the end of the chapter.

Question SA1 (K2)

Which of the following is true about the V-model?

a. It has the same steps as the waterfall model for software development.
b. It is referred to as a cyclical model for software development.
c. It enables the production of a working version of the system as early as possible.
d. It enables test planning to start as early as possible.

Question SA2 (K2)

Which of the following is true of iterative development?

a. It uses fully defined specifications from the start.
b. It involves the users in the testing throughout.
c. Changes to the system do not need to be formally recorded.
d. It is not suitable for developing websites.

Question SA3 (K1)

Which of the following is in the correct order (typically)?

a. Unit testing, system testing, acceptance testing, maintenance testing.
b. System testing, unit testing, acceptance testing, maintenance testing.
c. Acceptance testing, system testing, maintenance testing, unit testing.
d. Unit testing, maintenance testing, system testing, acceptance testing.

SOFTWARE DEVELOPMENT MODELS

A development life cycle for a software product involves capturing the initial requirements from the customer, expanding on these to provide the detail required for code production, writing the code and testing the product, ready for release.

A simple development model is shown in Figure 2.1. This is known traditionally as the waterfall model.

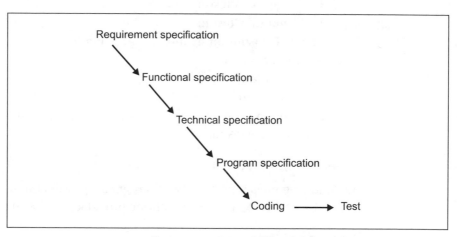

FIGURE 2.1   *Waterfall model*

The waterfall model in Figure 2.1 shows the steps in sequence where the customer requirements are progressively refined to the point where coding can take place. This type of model is often referred to as a linear or sequential model. Each work-product or activity is completed before moving on to the next.

In the waterfall model, testing is carried out once the code has been fully developed. Once this is completed, a decision can be made on whether the product can be released into the live environment.

This model for development shows how a fully tested product can be created, but it has a significant drawback: what happens if the product fails the tests? Let us look at a simple case study.

CASE STUDY – DEVELOPMENT PROCESS

In a factory environment producing rivets for an aircraft fuselage, checks are made by operators to assess the rivets on a conveyor belt. This assessment may reveal a percentage of the rivets to be defective. Usually this percentage is small, and does not result in the whole batch of rivets being rejected. Therefore the bulk of the product can be released.

Consider now the same aircraft, but the product is the software controlling the display provided for the aircrew. If, at the point of testing, too many defects are found, what happens next? Can we release just parts of the system?

In the waterfall model, the testing at the end serves as a quality check. The product can be accepted or rejected at this point. As we saw in the case of rivet production, a single point of quality checking may be acceptable, assuming that most rivets pass the quality check.

In software development, however, it is unlikely that we can simply reject the parts of the system found to be defective, and release the rest. The nature of software functionality is such that removal of software is often not a clean-cut activity – this action could well cause other areas to function incorrectly. It may even cause the system to become unusable.

In addition, we may not be able to choose not to deliver anything at all. The commercial and financial effects of this course of action could be substantial.

What is needed is a process which assures quality throughout the development life cycle. At every stage, a check should be made that the work-product for that stage meets its objectives. This is a key point, work-product evaluation taking place at the point where the product has been declared complete by its creator. If the work-product passes its evaluation (test), we can progress to the next stage in confidence. In addition, finding problems at the point of creation should make fixing any problems cheaper than fixing them at a later stage. This is the cost escalation model, described in Chapter 1.

The checks throughout the life cycle include verification and validation.

Verification – checks that the work-product meets the requirements set out for it. An example of this would be to ensure that a website being built follows the guidelines for making websites usable by as many people as possible. Verification helps to ensure that we are building the product in the right way.

Validation – changes the focus of work-product evaluation to evaluation against user needs. This means ensuring that the behaviour of the work-product matches the customer needs as defined for the project. For example, for the same website above, the guidelines may have been written with people familiar with websites in mind. It may be that this website is also intended for novice users. Validation would include these users checking that they too can use the website easily. Validation helps to ensure that we are building the right product as far as the users are concerned.

There are two types of development model which facilitate early work-product evaluation.

The first is an extension to the waterfall model, known as the V-model. The second is a cyclical model, where the coding stage often begins once the initial user needs have been captured. Cyclical models are often referred to as iterative models.

We will consider first the V-model.

V-model

There are many variants of the V-model. One of these is shown in Figure 2.2.

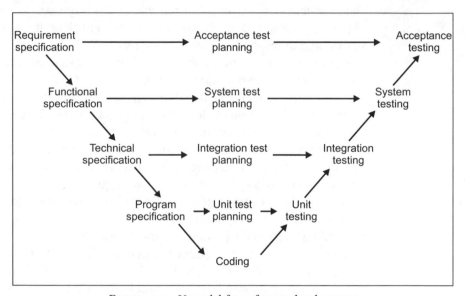

FIGURE 2.2 *V-model for software development*

As for the waterfall model, the left-hand side of the model focuses on elaborating the initial requirements, providing successively more technical detail as the development progresses. In the model shown, these are:

- Requirement specification – capturing of user needs.
- Functional specification – definition of functions required to meet user needs.
- Technical specification – technical design of functions identified in the functional specification.
- Program specification – detailed design of each module or unit to be built to meet required functionality.

These specifications could be reviewed to check for the following:

- Conformance to the previous work-product (so in the case of the functional specification, verification would include a check against the requirement specification).
- That there is sufficient detail for the subsequent work-product to be built correctly (again, for the functional specification, this would include a check that there is sufficient information in order to create the technical specification).
- That it is testable – is the detail provided sufficient for testing the work-product?

Formal methods for reviewing documents are discussed in Chapter 3.

The middle of the V-model shows that planning for testing should start with each work-product. Thus, using the requirement specification as an example, acceptance testing would be planned for, right at the start of the development. Test planning is discussed in more detail in Chapter 5.

The right-hand side focuses on the testing activities. For each work-product, a testing activity is identified. These are shown in Figure 2.2:

- Testing against the requirement specification takes place at the acceptance testing stage.
- Testing against the functional specification takes place at the system testing stage.
- Testing against the technical specification takes place at the integration testing stage.
- Testing against the program specification takes place at the unit testing stage.

This allows testing to be concentrated on the detail provided in each work-product, so that defects can be identified as early as possible in the life cycle, when the work-product has been created. The different stages of testing are discussed later.

Remembering that each stage must be completed before the next one can be started, this approach to software development pushes validation of the system by the user representatives right to the end of the life cycle. If the customer needs were not captured accurately in the requirements specification, or if they change, then these issues may not be uncovered until the user testing is carried out. As we saw in Chapter 1, fixing problems at this stage could be very costly; in addition, it is possible that the project could be cancelled altogether.

Iterative development models

Let us now look at a different model for software development – iterative development. This is one where the requirements do not need to be fully defined before coding can start. Instead, a working version of the product is built, in a series of stages, or iterations – hence the name iterative development. Each stage encompasses requirements definition, design, code and test. This is shown diagrammatically in Figure 2.3.

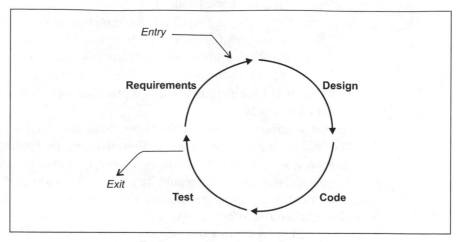

FIGURE 2.3 *Iterative development*

This type of development is often referred to as cyclical – we go 'round the development cycle a number of times', within the project. The project will have a defined timescale and cost. Within this, the cycles will be defined. Each cycle will also have a defined timescale and cost. The cycles are commonly referred to as time-boxes. For each time-box, a requirement is defined and a version of the code is produced, which will allow testing by the user representatives. At the end of each time-box, a decision is made on what extra functionality needs to be created for the next iteration. This process is then repeated until a fully working system has been produced.

A key feature of this type of development is the involvement of user representatives in the testing. Having the users represented throughout minimizes the risk of developing an unsatisfactory product. The user representatives are empowered to request changes to the software, to meet their needs.

This approach to software development can pose problems, however.

The lack of formal documentation makes it difficult to test. To counter this, developers may use test-driven development. This is where functional tests are written first, and code is then created and tested. It is reworked until it passes the tests.

In addition, the environment may be such that developers make any changes required, without formally recording them. This approach could mean that changes cannot be traced back to the requirements or to the parts of the software which have changed. Thus, traceability as the project progresses is reduced. To mitigate this, a robust process must be put in place at the start of the project to manage these changes (often part of a configuration management process – this is discussed further in Chapter 5).

Another issue associated with changes is the amount of testing required to ensure that implementation of the changes does not cause unintended changes to other parts of the software (this is called regression testing, discussed later in this chapter).

 Forms of iterative development include prototyping, rapid application development (RAD) and agile software development. A proprietary methodology is the Rational Unified Process (RUP).

CHECK OF UNDERSTANDING

(1) What is meant by verification?

(2) What is meant by validation?

(3) Name three work-products typically shown in the V-model.

(4) Name three activities typically shown in the V model.

(5) Identify a benefit of the V-model.

(6) Identify a drawback of the V-model.

(7) Name three activities typically associated with an iterative model.

(8) Identify a significant benefit of an iterative model.

(9) List three challenges of an iterative development.

(10) List three types of iterative development.

(11) Compare the work-products in the V-model with those in an iterative model.

TEST LEVELS

For both types of development, testing plays a significant role. Testing helps to ensure that the work-products are being developed in the right way (verification) and that the product will meet the user needs (validation).

Characteristics of good testing across the development life cycle include:

- Early test design – In the V-model, we saw that test planning begins with the specification documents. This activity is part of the fundamental test process discussed in Chapter 1. After test planning, the documents would be analysed and test cases designed. This approach would ensure that testing starts with the development of the requirements, i.e. a proactive approach to testing is undertaken. Proactive approaches to test design are discussed further in Chapter 5. As we saw in iterative development, test-driven development may be adopted, pushing testing to the front of the development activity.

- Each work-product is tested – In the V-model, each document on the left is tested by an activity on the right. Each specification document is called the test basis, i.e. it is the basis on which tests are created. In iterative development, each release is tested before moving on to the next.

- Testers are involved in reviewing requirements before they are released – In the V-model, testers would be invited to review all documents from a testing perspective. Techniques for reviewing documents are outlined in Chapter 3.

In Figure 2.2, the test stages of the V-model are shown. They are often called test levels. The term test level provides an indication of the focus of the testing, and the types of problems it is likely to uncover. The typical levels of testing are:

- Unit (component) testing
- Integration testing
- System testing
- Acceptance testing

Each of these test levels will include tests designed to uncover problems specifically at that stage of development. These levels of testing can be applied to iterative development also. In addition, the levels may change depending on the system. For instance, if the system includes some software developed by external parties, or bought off the shelf, acceptance testing on these may be conducted before testing the system as a whole.

Let us now look at these levels of testing in more detail.

Unit testing

Before testing of the code can start, clearly the code has to be written. This is shown at the bottom of the V-model. Generally, the code is written in parts, or units. The units are usually constructed in isolation, for integration at a later stage. Units are also called programs, modules or components.

Unit testing is intended to ensure that the code written for the unit meets its specification, prior to its integration with other units.

In addition to checking conformance to the program specification, unit testing would also verify that all of the code that has been written for the unit can be executed. Instead of using the specification to decide on inputs and expected outputs, the developer would use the code that has been written for this. Testing based on code is discussed in detail in Chapter 4.

Unit testing is usually performed by the developer who wrote the code (and who may also have written the program specification). Defects found and fixed during unit testing are often not recorded.

Integration testing

Once the units have been written, the next stage would be to put them together to create the system. This is called integration. It involves building something large from a number of smaller pieces.

The purpose of integration testing is to expose defects in the interfaces and in the interactions between integrated components or systems.

Before integration testing can be planned, an integration strategy is required. This involves making decisions on how the system will be put together prior to testing. There are three commonly quoted integration strategies, as follows.

Big-bang integration

This is where all units are linked at once, resulting in a complete system. When testing of this system is conducted, it is difficult to isolate any errors found, because attention is not paid to verifying the interfaces across individual units.

This type of integration is generally regarded as a poor choice of integration strategy. It introduces the risk that problems may be discovered late in the project, where they are more expensive to fix.

Top-down integration Evaluation

This is where the system is built in stages, starting with components which call other components. Components which call others are usually placed above those that are called. Top-down integration testing will permit the tester to evaluate component interfaces, starting with those at the 'top'.

Let us look at the diagram in Figure 2.4 to explain this further.

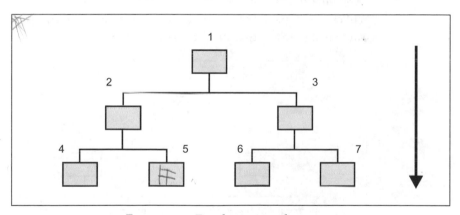

FIGURE 2.4   *Top-down control structure*

The control structure of a program can be represented in a chart. In Figure 2.4, component 1 can call components 2 and 3. Thus in the structure, component 1 is placed above components 2 and 3. Component 2 can call components 4 and 5. Component 3 can call components 6 and 7. Thus in the structure, components 2 and 3 are placed above components 4 and 5 and components 6 and 7, respectively.

In this chart, the order of integration might be:

- 1,2
- 1,3
- 2,4
- 2,5
- 3,6
- 3,7

Top-down integration testing requires that the interactions of each component must be tested when it is built. Those lower down in the hierarchy may not have been built or integrated yet. In Figure 2.4, in order to test component 1's interaction with component 2, it may be necessary to replace component 2 with a substitute since component 2 may not have been integrated yet. This is done by creating a skeletal implementation of the component, called a stub. A stub is a passive component, called by other components. In this example, stubs may be used to replace components 4 and 5, when testing component 2.

The use of stubs is commonplace in top-down integration, replacing components not yet integrated.

Bottom-up integration

This is the opposite of top-down integration and the components are integrated in a bottom-up order. This is shown in Figure 2.5.

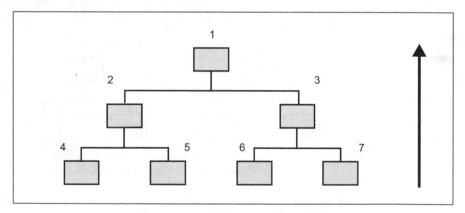

FIGURE 2.5   *Bottom-up integration*

The integration order might be:

- 4,2
- 5,2
- 6,3
- 7,3
- 2,1
- 3,1

So, in bottom-up integration, components 4–7 would be integrated before components 2 and 3. In this case, the components that may not be in place are those which actively call other components. As in top-down integration testing, they must be replaced by specially written components. When these special components call other components, they are called drivers. They are so called because, in the functioning program, they are active, controlling other components.

Components 2 and 3 could be replaced by drivers when testing components 4–7. They are generally more complex than stubs.

There may be more than one level of integration testing. For example:

- Component integration testing focuses on the interactions between software components and is done after component (unit) testing. This type of integration testing is usually carried out by developers.
- System integration testing focuses on the interactions between different systems and may be done after system testing of each individual system. For example, a trading system in an investment bank will interact with the stock exchange to get the latest prices for its stocks and shares on the international market. This type of integration testing is usually carried out by testers.

System testing

Having checked that the components all work together at unit level, the next step is to consider the functionality from an end-to-end perspective. This activity is called system testing.

System testing is necessary because many of the criteria for test selection at unit and integration testing result in the production of a set of test cases which are unrepresentative of the operating conditions in the live environment. Thus testing at these levels is unlikely to reveal errors due to interactions across the whole system, or those due to environmental issues.

System testing serves to correct this imbalance by focusing on the behaviour of the whole system/product as defined by the scope of a development project or programme, in a representative live environment. It is usually carried out by a team which is independent of the development process. The benefit of this independence is that an objective assessment of the system can be made, based on the specifications as written, and not the code.

In the V-model, the behaviour required of the system is documented in the functional specification. It defines what must be built to meet the requirements of the system. The functional specification should contain definitions of both the functional and non-functional requirements of the system.

A functional requirement is a requirement that specifies a function that a system or system component must perform. Functional requirements can be specific to a system. For instance, you would expect to be able to search for flights on a travel agent's website, whereas you would visit your online bank to check that you have sufficient funds to pay for the flight.

Thus functional requirements provide detail on what the application being developed will do.

Non-functional system testing looks at those aspects that are important but not directly related to what functions the system performs. These tend to be generic requirements, which can be applied to many different systems. In the example above, you can expect that both systems will respond to your inputs in a reasonable time frame, for instance. Typically, these requirements will consider both normal operations and behaviour under exceptional circumstances.

Thus non-functional requirements detail how the application will perform in use.

Examples of non-functional requirements include:

- Installability – installation procedures.

- Interoperability – operation of the application in different environments.
- Maintainability – ability to introduce changes to the system.
- Performance – expected normal behaviour.
- Load handling – behaviour of the system under increasing load.
- Stress handling – behaviour at the upper limits of system capability.
- Portability – use on different operating platforms.
- Recovery – recovery procedures on failure.
- Reliability – ability of the software to perform its required functions over time.
- Usability – ease with which users can engage with the system.

Note that security is regarded as a functional requirement in this syllabus.

The amount of testing required at system testing, however, can be influenced by the amount of testing carried out (if any) at the previous stages. In addition, the amount of testing advisable would also depend on the amount of verification carried out on the requirements (this is discussed further in Chapter 3).

Acceptance testing

The next step after system testing is often acceptance testing. The purpose of acceptance testing is to provide the end users with confidence that the system will function according to their expectations. Referring once more to the V-model, acceptance testing will be carried out using the requirement specification as a basis for test.

The requirement specification is typically the first document to be written, after initial capture of the user requirement. An example of a requirement could be to create a website which enables users to buy airline tickets online.

The subsequent documentation (functional, technical and program specifications) will expand on this in increasing levels of detail, in order to facilitate development of the system, as seen earlier. Thus, it is paramount that these requirements are fully documented and correct before further development activity is carried out. Again, this is the V-model approach. You may well be aware that having such an ideal set of requirements is a rare thing. This does not mean, however, that the need for correctness and completeness should be ignored. Techniques for verifying requirements are given in Chapter 3.

As for system testing, no reference is made to the code from which the system is constructed. Unlike system testing, however, the testing conducted here should be independent of any other testing carried out. Its key purpose is to demonstrate system conformance to the customer requirements. For instance, acceptance testing may assess the system's readiness for deployment and use.

Acceptance testing is often the responsibility of the customers or users of a system, although other project team members may be involved as well.

Typical forms of acceptance testing include the following:

- User acceptance testing – testing by user representatives to check that the system meets their business needs. This can include factory acceptance testing, where the system is tested by the users before moving it to their own site. Site acceptance testing could then be performed by the users at their own site.

- Operational acceptance testing – often called operational readiness testing. This involves checking that the processes and procedures are in place to allow the system to be used and maintained. This can include checking:
  + Back-up facilities
  + Procedures for disaster recovery
  + Training for end users
  + Maintenance procedures
  + Security procedures

- Contract and regulation acceptance testing
  + Contract acceptance testing – sometimes the criteria for accepting a system are documented in a contract. Testing is then conducted to check that these criteria have been met, before the system is accepted.
  + Regulation acceptance testing – in some industries, systems must meet governmental, legal or safety standards. Examples of these are the defence, banking and pharmaceutical industries.

- Alpha and beta testing
  + Alpha testing takes place at the developer's site – the operational system is tested whilst still at the developer's site by internal staff, before release to external customers.
  + Beta testing takes place at the customer's site – the operational system is tested by a group of customers, who use the product

at their own locations and provide feedback, before the system is released. This is often called ' field testing'.

CHECK OF UNDERSTANDING

(1) In the V-model, which document would be used as the test basis for unit testing? *requ doc*

(2) Describe three typical integration strategies.

(3) Identify why stubs and drivers are usually used.

(4) In the V-model, which document is used as the test basis for system testing? *functional spe*

(5) Compare a functional requirement with a non-functional requirement.

(6) List three non-functional requirements. *— fast man slow*

(7) What is the purpose of acceptance testing?

(8) In the V-model, what is the test basis for acceptance testing? *req doc*

(9) Identify three types of acceptance testing.

TESTING RELATED TO CHANGES

The previous sections detail the testing to be carried out at the different stages in the development life cycle. At any level of testing, it can be expected that defects will be discovered. When these are found and fixed, the quality of the system being delivered can be improved.

When a defect is detected and fixed then the changed software should be retested to confirm that the problem has been successfully removed. This is called confirmation testing. Note that when the developer removes the defect, this activity is called debugging, which is not a testing activity. Testing finds a defect, debugging fixes it.

The unchanged software should also be retested to ensure that no additional defects have been introduced as a result of changes to the software. This is called regression testing. Regression testing should also be carried out if the environment has changed.

Regression testing involves the creation of a set of tests which serve to demonstrate that the system works as expected. These would be run again many times over a testing project, when changes are made, as discussed above. This repetition of tests makes regression testing suitable for automation in many cases. Test automation is covered in detail in Chapter 6.

CHECK OF UNDERSTANDING

Which of the following is correct?

(a) Regression testing checks that a problem has been successfully addressed, whilst confirmation testing is done at the end of each release.

(b) Regression testing checks that all problems have been successfully addressed, whilst confirmation testing refers to testing individual fixes.

(c) Regression testing checks that fixes to errors do not introduce unexpected functionality into the system, whilst confirmation testing checks that fixes have been successful.

(d) Regression testing checks that all required testing has been carried out, whilst confirmation testing checks that each test is complete.

MAINTENANCE TESTING

For many projects (though not all) the system is eventually released into the live environment. Hopefully, once deployed, it will be in service as long as intended, perhaps for years or decades.

During this deployment, it may become necessary to change the system. Changes may be due to:

- Additional features being required.
- The system being migrated to a new operating platform.
- The system being retired – data may need to be migrated or archived.
- New faults being found.

Once changes have been made to the system, they will need to be tested (confirmation testing), and it also will be necessary to conduct regression testing to ensure that the rest of the system has not been adversely affected by the changes. Testing which takes place on a system which is in operation in the live environment is called maintenance testing.

All changes must be tested, and, ideally, all of the system should be subject to regression testing. In practice, this may not be feasible or cost effective. An understanding of the parts of the system which could be affected by the changes could reduce the amount of regression testing required. Working this out is termed impact analysis, i.e. analysing the impact of the changes on the system.

Impact analysis can be difficult for a system which has already been released. This is because the specifications may be out of date (or non-existent), and/or the original development team may have moved on to other projects, or left the organization altogether.

CHECK OF UNDERSTANDING

(1) What is the purpose of maintenance testing?

(2) Give examples of when maintenance testing would be necessary.

(3) What is meant by the term impact analysis?

SUMMARY

In this chapter we have explored the role of testing within the software development life cycle. We have looked at the basic steps in any development model, from understanding customer needs to delivery of the final product. These were built up into formally recognizable models, using distinct approaches to software development.

 The V-model, as we have seen, is a stepwise approach to software development, meaning that each stage in the model must be completed before the next stage can be started, if a strict implementation of the model is required. This is often the case in safety-critical developments. The V-model typically has the following work-products and activities:

(1) Requirement specification

(2) Functional specification

(3) Technical specification

(4) Program specification

(5) Code

(6) Unit testing

(7) Integration testing

(8) System testing

(9) Acceptance testing

Work-products 1–5 would be subject to verification, to ensure that they have been created following the rules set out. For example, the program specification would be assessed to ensure that it meets the requirements set out in the technical specification, and that it contains sufficient detail for the code to be produced.

In activities 6–9, the code is assessed progressively for compliance to user needs, as captured in the specifications for each level.

An iterative model for development has fewer steps, but involves the user from the start. These steps are typically:

(1) Define iteration requirement.

(2) Build iteration.

(3) Test iteration.

This sequence would be repeated for each iteration until an acceptable product has been developed.

An explanation of each of the test levels in the V-model was given. For unit testing the focus is the code within the unit itself, for integration testing it is the interfacing between units, for system testing it is the end-to-end functionality, and for acceptance testing it is the user perspective.

Finally, we looked at the testing required when a system has been released, but a change has become necessary – maintenance testing. We discussed the need for impact analysis in deciding how much regression testing to do after the changes have been implemented. This can pose an added challenge, if the requirements associated with the system are missing or have been poorly defined.

In the next chapter, techniques for improving requirements will be discussed.

Example examination questions with answers

E1. *K1 question*

Which of the following is usually the test basis for integration testing?

a. Program specification
b. Functional specification
c. Technical specification
d. Requirement specification

E2. *K2 question*

A top-down development strategy affects which level of testing most?

a. Component testing
b. Integration testing
c. System testing
d. User acceptance testing

E3. *K2 question*

Which of the following is a non-functional requirement?

a. The system will enable users to buy books.
b. The system will allow users to return books.
c. The system will ensure security of the customer details.
d. The system will allow up to 100 users to log in at the same time.

E4. *K1 question*

Which of the following are examples of iterative development models?

(i) V-model
(ii) Rapid Application Development model
(iii) Waterfall model
(iv) Agile development model

a. (i) and (ii)
b. (ii) and (iii)
c. (ii) and (iv)
d. (iii) and (iv)

E5. *K2 question*

Which of the following statements are true?

(i) For every development activity there is a corresponding testing activity.
(ii) Each test level has the same test objectives.
(iii) The analysis and design of tests for a given test level should begin after the corresponding development activity.
(iv) Testers should be involved in reviewing documents as soon as drafts are available in the development life cycle.

a. (i) and (ii)
b. (iii) and (iv)

c.   (ii) and (iii)

d.   (i) and (iv)

E6. K1 question

Which of the following is not true of regression testing?

a.   It can be carried out at each stage of the life cycle.

b.   It serves to demonstrate that the changed software works as intended.

c.   It serves to demonstrate that software has not been unintentionally changed.

d.   It is often automated.

Answers to questions in the chapter

SA1.   The correct answer is d.

SA2.   The correct answer is b.

SA3.   The correct answer is a.

Answers to example questions

E1. The correct answer is c.

Option (a) is used for unit testing. Option (b) is used for system testing and option (d) is used for acceptance testing.

E2. The correct answer is b.

The development strategy will affect the component testing (option (a)), in so far as it cannot be tested unless it has been built. Options (c) and (d) require the system to have been delivered; at these points the development strategy followed is not important to the tester. Option (b) needs knowledge of the development strategy in order to determine the order in which components will be integrated and tested.

E3. The correct answer is d.

The other options are functional requirements. Note that security is regarded as a functional requirement in this syllabus.

E4. The correct answer is c.

The other two models are sequential models.

E5. The correct answer is d.

Option (ii) is incorrect: each test level has a different objective. Option (iii) is also incorrect: test analysis and design should start once the documentation has been completed.

E6. The correct answer is b.

This is a definition of confirmation testing. The other three options are true of regression testing.

3 Static Testing

GEOFF THOMPSON

INTRODUCTION

This chapter provides an introduction to an important area of software testing – static techniques. Static techniques test software without executing it. They are therefore important because they can find errors and defects before code is executed and therefore earlier in the life cycle of a project, making corrections easier and cheaper to achieve than for the same defects found during test execution. Review techniques are central to the static testing approach, and in this chapter we will look at the alternative types of review and how they fit with the test process that was defined in Chapter 2.

The chapter also considers static analysis of the developed code, which is a technique for examining code without executing it to identify actual and potential problems. With the advances in coding languages and the legacy status of many older systems, static testing is often impossible to achieve manually, so our focus will therefore be on the types of static testing that can be completed using tools. In this chapter we focus on the techniques of static testing; the tools that are referred to are described in Chapter 6.

Learning objectives

The learning objectives for this chapter are listed below. You can confirm that you have achieved these by using the self-assessment questions at the start of the chapter, the 'Check of understanding' boxes distributed throughout the text, and the example examination questions provided at the end of the chapter. The chapter summary will remind you of the key ideas.

The sections are allocated a K number to represent the level of understanding required for that section; where an individual has a lower K number than the section as a whole this is indicated for that topic; for an explanation of the K numbers see the Introduction.

Reviews and the test process (K2)

- Recognize software work-products that can be examined by the different static techniques. (K1)
- Describe the importance and value of considering static techniques for the assessment of software work-products.
- Explain the difference between static and dynamic techniques.

Review process (K2)

- Recall the phases, roles and responsibilities of a typical formal review. (K1)
- Explain the differences between different types of review: informal review, technical review, walkthrough and inspection.
- Explain the factors for successful performance of reviews.

Static analysis by tools (K2)

- Describe the objective of static analysis and compare it with dynamic testing.
- Recall typical defects and errors identified by static analysis and compare them with reviews and dynamic testing. (K1)
- List typical benefits of static analysis. (K1)
- List typical code and design defects that may be identified by static analysis tools. (K1)

Self-assessment questions

The following questions have been designed to enable you to check your current level of understanding for the topics in this chapter. The answers are at the end of the chapter.

Question SA1 (K1)

One of the roles in a review is that of moderator, which of the following best describes this role?

- a. Plans the review, runs the review meeting and ensures that follow-up activities are completed.
- b. Allocates time in the plan, decides which reviews will take place and that the benefits are delivered.
- c. Writes the document to be reviewed, agrees that the document can be reviewed, and updates the document with any changes.
- d. Documents all issues raised in the review meeting, records problems and open points.

Question SA2 (K2)

Which of the following statements are correct for walkthroughs?

- (i) Often led by the author.
- (ii) Documented and defined results.
- (iii) All participants have defined roles.
- (iv) Used to aid learning.
- (v) Main purpose is to find defects.

- a. (i) and (v) are correct.
- b. (ii) and (iii) are correct.
- c. (i) and (iv) are correct.
- d. (iii) and (iv) are correct.

Question SA3 (K1)

What do static analysis tools analyse?

a. Design
b. Test cases
c. Requirements
d. Program code

BACKGROUND TO STATIC TECHNIQUES

Static testing techniques are those techniques that test software without executing the code. This includes both the testing of work-products other than code, typically requirements or specification documents, and the testing of code without actually executing it. The first of these is known as a review and is typically used to find and remove errors and ambiguities in documents before they are used in the development process, thus reducing one source of defects in the code; the second is known as static analysis, and it enables code to be analysed for structural defects or systematic programming weaknesses that may lead to defects.

Reviews are normally completed manually; static analysis is normally completed automatically using tools. The tools used for static analysis will be described in Chapter 6.

REVIEWS AND THE TEST PROCESS

A review is a systematic examination of a document by one or more people with the main aim of finding and removing errors. Giving a draft document to a colleague to read is the simplest example of a review, and one which can usually yield a larger crop of errors than we would have anticipated (see Chapter 5 regarding 'World view' to understand why).

Reviews can be used to test anything that is written or typed; this can include documents such as requirements specifications, system designs, code, test plans and test cases. Reviews represent the first form of testing that can take place during a software development life cycle, since the documents reviewed are normally ready long before the code has been written. The practice of testing specification documents by reviewing them early on in the life cycle helps to identify defects before they become part of the executable code, and so makes those defects cheaper and easier to remove. The same defect, if found during dynamic test execution, would incur the extra cost of initially creating and testing the defective code, diagnosing the source of the defect, correcting the problem and rewriting the code to eliminate the defect. Reviewing code against development standards can also prevent defects from appearing in test execution, though in this case, as the code has already been written, not all the additional costs and delays are avoided.

Important as cost and time saving are, though, there are also other important benefits of finding defects early in the life cycle, among them the following:

- Development productivity can be improved and timescales reduced because the correction of defects in early work-products will help to ensure that those work-products are clear and unambiguous. This should enable a developer to move more quickly through the process of writing code. Also, if defects are removed before they become executable code there will be fewer errors to find and fix during test execution.

- Testing costs and time can be reduced by removing the main delays in test execution, which arise when defects are found after they have become failures and the tester has to wait for a fix to be delivered. By reviewing the code and removing defects before they become failures the tester can move more swiftly through test execution.

- Reductions in lifetime costs can be achieved because fewer defects in the final software ensure that on-going support costs will be lower.

- Improved communication results as authors and their peers discuss and refine any ambiguous content discovered during review to ensure that all involved understand exactly what is being delivered.

The types of defects most typically found by reviews are:

- Deviations from standards either internally defined and managed or regulatory/legally defined by Parliament or perhaps a trade organization.

- Requirements defects – for example, the requirements are ambiguous, or there are missing elements.

- Design defects – for example, the design does not match the requirements.

- Insufficient maintainability – for example, the code is too complex too maintain.

- Incorrect interface specifications – for example, the interface specification does not match the design or the receiving or sending interface.

All reviews aim to find defects, but some types of review find certain types of defects more effectively and efficiently than others.

Review process

Review processes can vary widely in their level of formality, where formality relates to the level of structure and documentation associated with the activity. Some types of review are completely informal, while others are very formal. The decision on the appropriate level of formality for a review is usually based on combinations of the following factors:

- The maturity of the development process: the more mature the process is, the more formal reviews tend to be.

- Legal or regulatory requirements. These are used to govern the software development activities in certain industries, notably in safety-critical areas such as railway signalling, determine what kinds of review should take place.

- The need for an audit trail. Formal review processes ensure that it is possible to trace backwards throughout the software development life cycle. The level of formality in the types of review used can help to raise the level of audit trail.

Reviews can also have a variety of objectives, where the term 'review objective' identifies the main focus for a review. Typical review objectives include:

- Finding defects.
- Gaining understanding.
- Generating discussion.
- Decision making by consensus.

The way a review is conducted will depend on what its specific objective is, so a review aimed primarily at finding defects will be quite different from one that is aimed at gaining understanding of a document.

Basic review process

All reviews, formal and informal alike, exhibit the same basic elements of process:

- The document under review is studied by the reviewers.

- Reviewers identify issues or problems and inform the author either verbally or in a documented form, which might be as formal as raising a defect report or as informal as annotating the document under review.

- The author decides on any action to take in response to the comments and updates the document accordingly.

This basic process is always present, but in the more formal reviews it is elaborated to include additional stages and more attention to documentation and measurement.

Phases of a formal review

Reviews at the more formal end of the spectrum, such as technical reviews and inspections, share certain characteristics that differentiate them from the less formal reviews, of which walkthroughs are a typical example.

Figure 3.1 shows the key stages that characterize formal reviews.

The following list explains the key stages in more detail:

- Planning:
  - ✦ Selecting the personnel – ensuring that those selected can and will add value to the process. There is little point in selecting a reviewer who will agree with everything written by the author

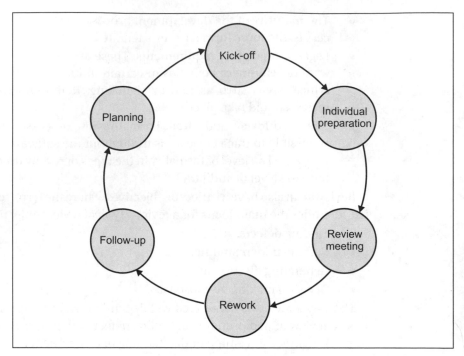

FIGURE 3.1 *Stages of a formal review*

without question. As a rule of thumb it is best to include some reviewers who are from a different part of the organization, who are known to be 'picky', and known to be dissenters. Reviews, like weddings, are enhanced by including 'something old, something new, something borrowed, something blue'. In this case 'something old' would be an experienced practitioner; 'something new' would be a new or inexperienced team member; 'something borrowed' would be someone from a different team; 'something blue' would be the dissenter who is hard to please. At the earliest stage of the process a review leader must be identified. This is the person who will coordinate all of the review activity.

✦ Allocating roles – each reviewer is given a role to provide them with a unique focus on the document under review. Someone in a tester role might be checking for testability and clarity of definition, while someone in a user role might look for simplicity and a clear relationship to business values. This approach ensures that, although all reviewers are working on the same document, each individual is looking at it from a different perspective.

✦ Defining the entry and exit criteria, especially for the most formal review types (e.g. inspection).

✦ Selecting the parts of documents to be reviewed (not always required; this will depend on the size of the document: a large document may need to be split into smaller parts and each part reviewed by a different person to ensure the whole document is reviewed fully).

- Kick-off: distributing documents; explaining the objectives, process and documents to the participants; and checking entry criteria (for more formal review types such as Inspections). This can be run as a meeting or simply by sending out the details to the reviewers. The method used will depend on timescales and the volume of information to pass on. A lot of information can be disseminated better by a meeting rather than expecting reviewers to read pages of text.

- Individual preparation: work done by each of the participants on their own before the review meeting, which would include reading the source documents, noting potential defects, questions and comments. This is a key task and may actually be time-boxed, e.g. participants may be given 2 hours to complete the preparation.

- Review meeting: this may include discussion regarding any defects found, or simply just a log of defects found. The more formal review types like inspections will have documented results or minutes. The meeting participants may simply note defects for the author to correct; they might also make recommendations for handling or correcting the defects. The approach taken will have been decided at the kick-off stage so that all participants are aware of what is required of them. The decision as to which approach to take may be based on one or all of the following factors:

  - Time available (if time is short the meeting may only collect defects).
  - Requirements of the author (if the author would like help in correcting defects).
  - Type of review (in an Inspection only the collection of defects is allowed – there is never any discussion).

- Rework: after a review meeting the author will have a series of defects to correct; correcting the defects is called rework. Basically the author will be fixing defects that were found and agreed as requiring a fix.

- Follow-up: the review leader will check that the agreed defects have been addressed and will gather metrics such as how much time was spent on the review and how many defects were found. The review leader will also check the exit criteria (for more formal review types such as Inspections) to ensure that they have been met.

Roles and responsibilities

The role of each reviewer is to look at documents belonging to them from their assigned perspective; this may include the use of checklists. For example, a checklist based on a particular perspective (such as user, maintainer, tester or operations) may be used, or a more general checklist (such as typical requirements problems) may be used to identify defects.

In addition to these assigned review roles the review process itself defines specific roles and responsibilities that should be fulfilled for formal reviews. They are:

- Manager: the manager decides on what is to be reviewed (if not already defined), ensures there is sufficient time allocated in the project plan for all of the required review activities, and determines if the review objectives have been met. Managers do not normally get involved in the actual review process unless they can add real value, e.g. they have technical knowledge key to the review.

- Moderator: the moderator is sometimes known as the review leader. This is the person who leads the review of the document or set of documents, including planning the review, running the meeting, and follow-ups after the meeting. If necessary, the moderator may mediate between the various points of view and is often the person upon whom the success of the review rests. The moderator will also make the final decision as to whether to release an updated document.

- Author: The author is the writer or person with chief responsibility for the development of the document(s) to be reviewed. The author will in most instances also take responsibility for fixing any agreed defects.

- Reviewers: These are individuals with a specific technical or business background (also called checkers or inspectors) who, after the necessary preparation, identify and describe findings (e.g. defects) in the product under review. As discussed above, reviewers should be chosen to represent different perspectives and roles in the review process and take part in any review meetings

- Scribe (or recorder): The scribe attends the review meeting and documents all of the issues and defects, problems and open points that were identified during the meeting.

An additional role not normally associated with reviews is that of the tester. Testers have a particular role to play in relation to document reviews. In their test analysis role they will be required to analyse a document to enable the development of tests. In analysing the document they will also review it, e.g. in starting to build end-to-end scenarios they will notice if there is a 'hole' in the requirements that will stop the business functioning, such as a process that is missing or some data that is not available at a given point. So effectively a tester can either be formally invited to review a document or may do so by default in carrying out the tester's normal test analysis role.

CHECK OF UNDERSTANDING

(1) Identify three benefits of reviews.

(2) What happens during the planning phase of a review?

(3) Who manages the review process?

Types of review

A single document may be subject to many different review types: for example, an informal review may be carried out before the document is subjected to a technical review or, depending on the level of risk, a technical review or inspection may take place before a walkthrough with a customer.

Figure 3.2 shows the different levels of formality by review type.

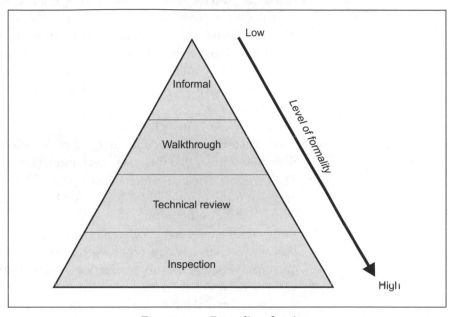

FIGURE 3.2 *Formality of reviews*

Each type of review has its own defining characteristics. We identify four review types to cover the spectrum of formality. These are usually known as:

(1) Informal review (least formal). Key characteristics:

- There is no formal process underpinning the review.
- The review may be documented but this is not required; many informal reviews are not documented.
- There may be some variations in the usefulness of the review depending on the reviewer, e.g. the reviewer does not have the technical skills but is just available to check quickly and ensure that the document makes sense.
- The main purpose is to find defects and this is an inexpensive way to achieve some limited benefit.
- The review may be implemented by pair programming (where one programmer reviews the code of the other 'pair programmer') or by a technical lead reviewing designs and code.

(2) Walkthrough. Key characteristics:

- The meeting is led by the author of the document under review and attended by members of the author's peer group.
- Review sessions are open ended and may vary in practice from quite informal to very formal.
- Preparation by reviewers before the walkthrough meeting, production of a review report or a list of findings, and appointment of a scribe who is not the author are all optional components that are sometimes present.
- The main purposes are to enable learning about the content of the document under review, to help team members gain an understanding of the content of the document, and to find defects.
- Walkthroughs typically explore scenarios, or conduct dry runs of code or process.

(3) Technical review. Key characteristics:
- Technical reviews are documented and use a well-defined defect-detection process that includes peers and technical experts.
- The review is usually performed as a peer review without management participation and is ideally led by a trained moderator who is not the author.
- Reviewers prepare for the review meeting, optionally using checklists, and prepare a review report with a list of findings.
- Technical reviews may vary in practice from the quite informal to very formal and have a number of purposes, including: discussion, decision making, evaluation of alternatives, finding defects, solving technical problems and checking conformance to specifications and standards.

(4) Inspection (most formal). Key characteristics:
- Inspections are led by a trained moderator who is not the author and usually involve peer examination of a document; individual inspectors work within defined roles.
- The inspection process is formal, based on rules and checklists, and uses entry and exit criteria.
- Pre-meeting preparation is essential, which would include reading of any source documents to ensure consistency.
- An inspection report, with a list of findings, is produced, which includes metrics that can be used to aid improvements to the process as well as correcting defects in the document under review.
- After the meeting a formal follow-up process is used to ensure that corrective action is completed and timely.
- The main purpose is to find defects, and process improvement may be a secondary purpose.

In reality the lines between the review types often get blurred and what is seen as a technical review in one company may be seen as an inspection in another. The above is the 'classic view' of reviews. The key for each company is to agree the objectives and benefits of the reviews that they plan to carry out.

Success factors for reviews

When measuring the success of a particular review the following suggested success factors should be considered:

- Each review should have a clearly predefined and agreed objective and the right people should be involved to ensure the objective is met. For example, in an Inspection each reviewer will have a defined role and therefore needs the experience to fulfil that role.
- Any defects found are welcomed, and expressed objectively, and the review leader has ensured that the people issues and psychological aspects are dealt with (e.g. making it a positive experience for the author and all participants).
- Review techniques (both formal and informal) that are suitable to the type and level of software work-products and reviewers (this is especially important in inspections).
- Checklists or roles should be used, where appropriate, to increase effectiveness of defect identification; for example, in an inspection, roles such as data entry clerk or technical architect may be required to review a particular document.
- Management support is essential for a good review process (e.g. by incorporating adequate time for review activities in project schedules).
- There should be an emphasis on learning and process improvement.

Other more quantitative approaches to success measurement could also be used:

- How many defects found.
- Time taken to review/inspect.
- Percentage of project budget used/saved.

In his original paper on the benefits of inspections in 1976, Michael Fagan of IBM, who developed the Fagan Inspection Method, reported a 23 per cent increase in 'coding productivity alone' by using inspections. Success can be measured in many ways; however, the key is to keep measuring to ensure success is still being achieved and, more importantly, reported to a wider audience.

CHECK OF UNDERSTANDING

(1) Compare the differences between a walkthrough and an inspection.

(2) Name three characteristics of a walkthrough.

(3) Identify at least five success factors for a review.

STATIC ANALYSIS BY TOOLS

Like reviews, static analysis looks for defects without executing the code. However, unlike reviews static analysis is carried out once the code has been written. Its objective is to find defects in software source code and software models.

Source code is any series of statements written in some human-readable computer programming language which can then be converted to equivalent computer executable code – it is normally generated by the developer.

A software model is an image of the final solution developed using techniques such as Unified Modeling Language (UML); it is normally generated by a software designer.

Static analysis can find defects that are hard to find during test execution by analysing the program code e.g. instructions to the computer can be in the form of control flow graphs (how control passes between modules) and data flows (ensuring data is identified and correctly used).

The value of static analysis is:

- Early detection of defects prior to test execution. As with reviews, the earlier the defect is found, the cheaper and easier it is to fix.

- Early warning about suspicious aspects of the code or design, by the calculation of metrics, such as a high-complexity measure. If code is too complex it can be more prone to error or less dependent on the focus given to the code by developers. If they understand that the code has to be complex then they are more likely to check and double check that it is correct; however, if it is unexpectedly complex there is a higher chance that there will be a defect in it.

- Identification of defects not easily found by dynamic testing, such as development standard breaches as well as detecting dependencies and inconsistencies in software models, such as links or interfaces that were either incorrect or unknown before static analysis was carried out.

- Improved maintainability of code and design. By carrying out static analysis, defects will be removed that would otherwise have increased the amount of maintenance required after 'go live'. It can also recognize complex code which if corrected will make the code more understandable and therefore easier to maintain.

- Prevention of defects. By identifying the defect early in the life cycle it is a lot easier to identify why it was there in the first place (root cause analysis) than during test execution, thus providing information on possible process improvement that could be made to prevent the same defect appearing again.

Typical defects discovered by static analysis tools include:

- Referencing a variable with an undefined value, e.g. using a variable as part of a calculation before the variable has been given a value.
- Inconsistent interface between modules and components, e.g. module X requests three values from module Y, which has only two outputs.
- Variables that are never used. This is not strictly an error, but if a programmer declares a variable in a program and does not use it, there is a chance that some intended part of the program has inadvertently been omitted,
- Unreachable (dead) code. This means lines of code that cannot be executed because the logic of the program does not provide any path in which that code is included.
- Programming standards violations, e.g. if the standard is to add comments only at the end of the piece of code, but there are notes throughout the code, this would be a violation of standards.
- Security vulnerabilities, e.g. password structures that are not secure.
- Syntax violations of code and software models, e.g. incorrect use of the programming or modelling language.

Static analysis tools add the greatest value when used during component and integration testing. This will normally involve checking by developers against predefined rules or development standards and by designers during software modelling.

A static analysis tool runs automatically and reports all defects it identifies, some of which may be insignificant and require little or no work to correct, whilst others could be critical and need urgent correction. These defects therefore require strong management to ensure that the full benefit is obtained from using the tool in the first place.

Software compilers are computer programs (or a set of programs) that translate codes written in one computer language (the source language) into another computer language (the target language). As part of the compile process certain static analysis can be undertaken which will identify some defects and provide the calculation of software metrics.

Static analysis tools are explained in Chapter 6.

CHECK OF UNDERSTANDING

(1) What is static analysis looking for?

(2) Name the five benefits of static analysis.

(3) What is the name of the type of defect that relates to password checks?

SUMMARY

In this chapter we have looked at how review techniques and static analysis fit within the test process defined in Chapter 2. We have understood that a review is a static test, i.e. it is a test carried out without executing any code (by reading and commenting on any document (work-product) such as a requirements specification, a piece of code or a test plan/test case). We have also looked at the different types of review techniques available, such as walkthroughs and inspections, as well as spending time understanding the benefits of reviews themselves.

Reviews vary in formality. The formality governs the amount of structure and documentation that surround the review itself.

To obtain the most benefit from reviews, they should be carried out as early in the project life cycle as possible, preferably as soon as the document to be reviewed has been written and definitely, in the case of work-products such as requirement specifications and designs, before any code is written or executed. The roles of the participant reviewers need to be defined and, in the more structured review techniques, written output from reviews is expected

We have learnt that static analysis is checking the developed software code before it is executed, checking for defects such as unreachable (dead code) and the misuse of development standards. We have also learnt that static analysis is best carried out using tools, which are described in detail in Chapter 6.

Like reviews, the best benefits of static analysis are realized when it is carried out as soon as possible after the code is written.

Example Examination Questions with Answers

E1. K1 question

Which of the following is most likely to be a benefit of using static techniques?

a.   Fewer performance defects.
b.   Productivity improvements in the development process.
c.   More efficient regression testing.
d.   Quick return on investment in static analysis tools.

E2. K2 question

Which of the following has the typical formal review activities in the correct sequence?

a.   Kick-off, review meeting, planning, follow-up.
b.   Kick-off, planning, review meeting, re-work.
c.   Planning, kick-off, individual preparation, review meeting.
d.   Planning, individual preparation, follow-up, re-work.

E3. K2 question

Which of the following statements are true?

(i)   Defects are likely to be found earlier in the development process by using reviews rather than static analysis.
(ii)   Walkthroughs require code but static analysis does not require code.
(iii)   Informal reviews can be performed on code and specifications.
(iv)   Dynamic techniques are generally used before static techniques.
(v)   Dynamic techniques can only be used after code is ready to be executed.

a.   (i), (ii), (vi).
b.   (ii), (iii), (v).
c.   (i), (iv), (v).
d.   (i), (iii), (v).

E4. K1 question

Which of the following are static techniques?

a.   Walkthrough.
b.   State transition testing.
c.   Decision table testing.
d.   Statement testing.

E5. K1 question

Which one of the following roles is typically used in a review?

a.   Champion.
b.   Author.

c.   Project sponsor.

d.   Custodian.

E6. K2 question

Which of the following is most likely to be performed by developers?

a.   Technical review of a functional specification.

b.   Walkthrough of a requirements document.

c.   Informal review of a program specification.

d.   Static analysis of a software model.

Answers to questions in the chapter

SA1.   The correct answer is a.

SA2.   The correct answer is c.

SA3.   The correct answer is d.

Answers to example questions

E1. The correct answer is b.

Although the other options might be seen as benefits they are not amongst the most likely benefits. Option (b) is the benefit that is most likely to be realized.

E2. The correct answer is c.

The correct sequence is: planning, kick-off, individual preparation, review meeting, re-work, follow-up. All of the other options have either the activities in the wrong order or activities missing from the strict flow.

E3. The correct answer is d.

The other answers are incorrect because:

ii. Walkthroughs do not require code and static analysis does require code.

iv. Static techniques do not execute the code and therefore can be run before and after the code is ready for execution.

E4. The correct answer is a.

Options (b), (c), and (d) are all dynamic test techniques.

E5. The correct answer is b.

The Author is the only role that is typically used in a review. A Champion might sponsor the review process but is not a defined role within an actual review; a Project Sponsor, if technically competent, might be asked to play a defined role within the review process, but whilst using that role they will not be a Project Sponsor; finally, a Custodian might ensure the results are stored safely but would not be involved in the actual review itself.

E6. The correct answer is d.

Static analysis is done almost exclusively by developers. The other review types would be performed using a combination of developers, testers and other interested stakeholders.

4 Test Design Techniques

BRIAN HAMBLING

INTRODUCTION

This chapter covers the very large topic of test case design techniques. Beginning with an introduction to the key terms and the basic process of creating a suite of tests for execution, the chapter explores the three categories of test case design techniques: specification-based, structure-based and experience-based. In each case specific techniques are explained and examples are given of their use. A final section on the selection of techniques completes the chapter.

Learning objectives

The learning objectives for this chapter are listed below. You can confirm that you have achieved these by using the self-assessment questions at the start of the chapter, the 'Check of understanding' boxes distributed throughout the text, and the example examination questions provided at the end of the chapter. The chapter summary will remind you of the key ideas.

The sections are allocated a K number to represent the level of understanding required for that section; where an individual topic has a lower K number than the section as a whole this is indicated for that topic; for an explanation of the K numbers see the Introduction.

Identifying test conditions and designing test cases (K3)
- Differentiate between a test design specification, test case specification and test procedure specification. (K1)
- Compare the terms 'test condition', 'test case' and 'test procedure'. (K2)

- Write test cases showing a clear traceability to the requirements; and containing an expected result.
- Translate test cases into a well-structured test procedure specification at a level of detail relevant to the knowledge of the testers.
- Write a test execution schedule for a given set of test cases, considering prioritization, and technical and logical dependencies.

Categories of test design techniques (K2)
- Recall reasons that both specification-based (black-box) and structure-based (white-box) approaches to test case design are useful, and list the common techniques for each. (K1)
- Explain the characteristics and differences between specification-based testing, structure-based testing and experience-based testing.

Specification-based or black-box techniques (K3)

- Write test cases from given software models using the following test design techniques:
  - equivalence partitioning;
  - boundary value analysis;
  - decision tables;
  - state transition diagrams.
- Understand the main purpose of each of the four techniques, what level and type of testing could use the technique, and how coverage may be measured. (K2)
- Understand the concept of use case testing and its benefits. (K2)

Structure-based or white-box techniques (K3)

- Describe the concept and importance of code coverage. (K2)
- Explain the concepts of statement and decision coverage, and understand that these concepts can also be used at other test levels than component testing (e.g. on business procedures at system level). (K2)
- Write test cases from given control flows using the test design techniques of statement testing and decision testing.
- Assess statement and decision coverage for completeness.

Experience-based techniques (K2)

- Recall reasons for writing test cases based on intuition, experience and knowledge about common defects. (K1)
- Compare experience-based techniques with specification-based testing techniques.

Choosing test techniques (K2)

- List the factors that influence the selection of the appropriate test design technique for a particular kind of problem, such as the type of system, risk, customer requirements, models for use case modelling, requirements models or tester knowledge.

Self-assessment questions

The following questions have been designed to enable you to check your current level of understanding for the topics in this chapter. The answers are at the end of the chapter. If you struggled with the K3 question you probably need more practice with applying the techniques; you can get this by working through the examples and exercises and attempting the additional practice questions at the end of the chapter. If you struggled with the K2 question it suggests that, while your recall of key ideas might be reasonable, your ability to apply the ideas needs developing. You need to study this chapter carefully and be careful to recognize all the connections between individual topics.

Question SA1 (K1)

Which of the following defines the expected result of a test?

a. Test case
b. Test procedure
c. Test execution schedule
d. Test condition

Question SA2 (K2)

Which of the following are **most** characteristic of structure-based testing?

(i) Information about how the software is constructed is used to derive test cases.
(ii) Statement coverage and/or decision coverage can be measured for existing test cases.
(iii) The knowledge and experience of people are used to derive test cases.
(iv) Test cases are derived from a model or specification of the system.

a. (i) and (ii)
b. (ii) and (iii)
c. (ii) and (iv)
d. (i) and (iii)

Question SA3 (K3)

A system is designed to accept values of examination marks as follows:

Fail	0–39 inclusive
Pass	40–59 inclusive
Merit	60–79 inclusive
Distinction	80–100 inclusive

In which of the following sets of values are all values in different equivalence partitions?

a. 25, 40, 60, 75
b. 0, 45, 79, 87
c. 35, 40, 59, 69
d. 25, 39, 60, 81

TEST CONDITIONS, TEST CASES AND TEST PROCEDURES

The specification of test cases is the second step in the fundamental test process (FTP) defined in the Introduction. The terms specification and design are used interchangeably in this context; in this section we discuss the creation of test cases by design.

The design of tests comprises three main steps:

(1) Identify test conditions.

(2) Specify test cases.

(3) Specify test procedures.

Our first task is to become familiar with the terminology.

> **A test condition – an item or event of a component or system that could be verified by one or more test cases, e.g. a function, transaction, feature, quality attribute, or structural element.**

In other words, a test condition is some characteristic of our software that we can check with a test or a set of tests.

> **A test case – a set of input values, execution preconditions, expected results and execution postconditions, developed for a particular objective or test condition, such as to exercise a particular program path or to verify compliance with a specific requirement.**

In other words, a test case: gets the system to some starting point for the test (execution preconditions); then applies a set of input values that should achieve a given outcome (expected result), and leaves the system at some end point (execution postcondition).

Our test design activity will generate the set of input values and we will predict the expected outcome by, for example, identifying from the specification what should happen when those input values are applied.

We have to define what state the system is in when we start so that it is ready to receive the inputs and we have to decide what state it is in after the test so that we can check that it ends up in the right place.

> **A test procedure specification – a sequence of actions for the execution of a test.**

A test procedure therefore identifies all the necessary actions in sequence to execute a test. Test procedure specifications are often called test scripts (or sometimes manual test scripts to distinguish them from the automated scripts that control test execution tools, introduced in Chapter 6).

So, going back to our three step process above, we:

(1) decide on a test condition, which would typically be a small section of the specification for our software under test;

(2) design a test case that will verify the test condition;

(3) write a test procedure to execute the test, i.e. get it into the right starting state, input the values, and check the outcome.

In spite of the technical language, this is quite a simple set of steps. Of course we will have to carry out a very large number of these simple steps to test a whole system, but the basic process is still the same. To test a whole system we write a test execution schedule, which puts all the individual test procedures in the right sequence and sets up the system so that they can be run.

The best way to clarify the process is to work through a simple example.

TEST CASE DESIGN BASICS

Suppose we have a system which contains the following specification for an input screen:

1.2.3 The input screen shall have three fields: a title field with a drop-down selector; a surname field which can accept up to 20 alphabetic characters and the hyphen (-) character; a first name field which can accept up to 20 alphabetic characters. All alphabetic characters shall be case insensitive. All fields must be completed. The data is validated when the Enter key is pressed. If the data is valid the system moves on to the job input screen; if not, an error message is displayed.

This specification enables us to define test conditions; for example, we could define a test condition for the surname field (i.e. it can accept up to 20 alphabetic characters and the hyphen (-) character) and define a set of test cases to test that field.

To test the surname field we would have to navigate the system to the appropriate input screen, select a title, tab to the surname field (all this would be setting the test precondition), enter a value (the first part of the set of input values), tab to the first name field and enter a value (the second part of the set of input values which we need because all fields must be completed), then press the Enter key. The system should either move on to the job input screen (if the data we input was valid) or display an error message (if the input data was not valid). Of course, we would need to test both of these cases.

The preceding paragraph is effectively the test procedure, though we might lay it out differently for real testing.

A good test case needs some extra information. First, it should be traceable back to the test condition and the element of the specification that it is testing; we can do this by applying the specification reference to the test, e.g. by identifying this test as T1.2.3.1 (because it is the first test associated with specification element 1.2.3). Secondly, we would need to add a specific value for the input, say 'Hambling' and 'Brian'. Finally we would specify that the system should move to the job input screen when 'Enter' is pressed.

TEST CASE DESIGN EXAMPLE

As an example, we could key in the following test cases:

Mr	Hambling	Brian
Ms	Samaroo	Angelina
Ms	Simmonite	Compo
Mr	Hyde-White	Wilfred

All these would be valid test cases; even though Compo Simmonite was an imaginary male character in a TV series, the input is correct according to the specification.

We should also test some invalid inputs, such as:

Mr	Thompson1	Geoff
Mr	"Morgan"	Peter
Mr	Williams	'Pete'

There are many more possibilities that infringe the rules in the specification, but these should serve to illustrate the point. You may be thinking that this simple specification could generate a very large number of test cases – and you would be absolutely right. One of our aims in using systematic test case design techniques will be to cut down the number of tests we need to run to achieve a given level of confidence in the software we are testing.

The test procedure would need to add some details along the following lines:

(1) Select the <Name or Personal Details> option from the main menu.

(2) Select the 'input' option from the <Name or Personal Details> menu.

(3) Select 'Mr' from the 'Title' drop-down menu.

(4) Check that the cursor moves to the 'surname' field.

(5) Type in 'Hambling' and press the tab key once; check that the cursor moves to the 'first name' field.

(6) Type in 'Brian' and press the Enter key.

(7) Check that the Job Input screen is displayed.

(8) . . .

That should be enough to demonstrate what needs to be defined, and also how slow and tedious such a test would be to run, and we have only completed one of the test cases so far!

The test procedure would collect together all the test cases related to this specification element so that they can all be executed together as a block;

there would be several to test valid and non-valid inputs, as you have seen in the example.

In the wider process (the FTP) we would move on to the test execution step next. In preparation for execution the test execution schedule collects together all the tests and sequences them, taking into account any priorities (highest priority tests would be run first) and any dependencies between tests. For example, it would make sense to do all the tests on the input screen together and to do all the tests that use input data afterwards; that way we get the input screen tests to do the data entry that we will need for the later tests. There might also be technical reasons why we run tests in a particular sequence; for example, a test of the password security needs to be done at the beginning of a sequence of tests because we need to be able to get into the system to run the other tests.

THE IDEA OF TEST COVERAGE

Test coverage is a very important idea because it provides a quantitative assessment of the extent and quality of testing. In other words, it answers the question 'how much testing have you done?' in a way that is not open to interpretation. Statements such as 'I'm nearly finished', or 'I've done 2 weeks' testing' or 'I've done everything in the test plan' generate more questions than they answer. They are statements about how much testing has been done or how much effort has been applied to testing, rather than statements about how effective the testing has been or what has been achieved. We need to know about test coverage for two very important reasons:

- It provides a quantitative measure of the quality of the testing that has been done by measuring what has been achieved.
- It provides a way of estimating how much more testing needs to be done. Using quantitative measures we can set targets for test coverage and measure progress against them.

Statements like 'I have tested 75 per cent of the decisions' or 'I've tested 80 per cent of the requirements' provide useful information. They are neither subjective nor qualitative; they provide a real measure of what has actually been tested. If we apply coverage measures to testing based on priorities, which are themselves based on the risks addressed by individual tests, we will have a reliable, objective and quantified framework for testing.

Test coverage can be applied to any systematic technique; in this chapter we will apply it to specification-based techniques to measure how much of the functionality has been tested, and to structure-based techniques to measure how much of the code has been tested. Coverage measures may be part of the completion criteria defined in the test plan (step 1 of the FTP) and used to determine when to stop testing in the final step of the FTP.

CHECK OF UNDERSTANDING

(1) What defines the process of test execution?

(2) Briefly compare a test case and a test condition.

(3) Which document identifies the sequence in which tests are executed?

(4) Describe the purpose of a test coverage measure.

CATEGORIES OF TEST CASE DESIGN TECHNIQUES

There are very many ways to design test cases. Some are general, others are very specific. Some are very simple to implement, others are difficult and complex to implement. The many excellent books published on software testing techniques every year testify to the rate of development of new and interesting approaches to the challenges that confront the professional software tester.

There is, however, a collection of test case design techniques that has come to be recognized as the most important ones for a tester to learn to apply, and these have been selected as the representatives of test case design for the Foundation Certificate, and hence for this book.

The test case design techniques we will look at are grouped into three categories:

- Those based on deriving test cases directly from a specification or a model of a system or proposed system, known as specification-based or black-box techniques.
- Those based on deriving test cases directly from the code written to implement a system, known as structure-based, or white-box techniques.
- Those based on deriving test cases from the tester's experience of similar systems and general experience of testing, known as experience-based techniques.

It is convenient to categorize techniques for test case design in this way (it is easier for you to remember, for one thing) but do not assume that these are the only categories or the only techniques; there are many more that can be added to the tester's 'tool kit' over time.

The category now known as specification-based used to be known as 'black-box', mainly because the techniques in it take a view of the system that does not need to know what is going on 'inside the box'. Those of us born in the first half of the 20th century will recognize 'black box' as the name of anything technical that you can use but about which you know nothing or next to nothing. The name has been changed relatively recently to provide a more descriptive title for those who may not find the 'black-box' image helpful. The natural alternative to 'black box' is 'white box'. White came originally from being 'not black', but some people argued that you need to be able to see inside the box (to see the structure) and a white box would be just as opaque as a black box – hence 'glass box'.

Experience-based testing was not really treated as 'proper' testing in testing prehistory, so it was given a disdainful name such as ' ad hoc'; the implication that this was not a systematic approach was enough to exclude it from many discussions about testing. Both the intellectual climate and the sophistication of experience-based techniques have moved on from those early days. It is worth bearing in mind that many systems are still tested in an experience-based way, partly because the systems are not specified in enough detail or in a sufficiently structured way to enable other categories of technique to be applied, or because neither the development team nor the testing team have been trained in the use of specification-based or structure-based techniques.

Before we look at these categories in detail, think for a moment about what we are trying to achieve. We want to try to check that a system does everything that its specification says it should do and nothing else. In practice the 'nothing else' is the hardest part and generates the most tests; that is because there are far more ways of getting anything wrong than there are ways of getting it right. Even if we just concentrate on testing that the system does what it is supposed to do, we will still generate a very large number of tests. This will be expensive and time consuming, which means it probably will not happen, so we need to ensure that our testing is as efficient as possible. As you will see, the best techniques do this by creating the smallest set of tests that will achieve a given objective, and they do that by taking advantage of certain things we have learned about testing; for example, that defects tend to cluster in interesting ways.

Bear this in mind as we take a closer look at the categories of test case design techniques.

SPECIFICATION-BASED OR BLACK-BOX TECHNIQUES

The main thing about specification-based techniques is that they derive test cases directly from the specification or from some other kind of model of what the system should do. The source of information on which to base testing is known as the 'test basis'. If a test basis is well defined and adequately structured we can easily identify test conditions from which test cases can be derived.

The most important point about specification-based techniques is that specifications or models do not (and should not) define how a system should achieve the specified behaviour when it is built; it is a specification of the required (or at least desired) behaviour. One of the hard lessons that software engineers have learned from experience is that it is important to separate the definition of what a system should do (a specification) from the definition of how it should work (a design). This separation allows the two specialist groups (testers for specifications and designers for design) to work independently so that we can later check that they have arrived at the same place, i.e. they have together built a system and tested that it works according to its specification.

If we set up test cases so that we check that desired behaviour actually occurs then we are acting independently of the developers. If they have misunderstood the specification or chosen to change it in some way without telling anyone then their implementation will deliver behaviour that is different from what the model or specification said the system behaviour should be. Our test, based solely on the specification, will therefore fail and we will have uncovered a problem.

Bear in mind that not all systems are defined by a detailed formal specification. In some cases the model we use may be quite informal. If there is no specification at all, the tester may have to build a model of the proposed system, perhaps by interviewing key stakeholders to understand what their expectations are. However formal or informal the model is, and however it is built, it provides a test basis from which we can generate tests systematically.

Remember, also, that the specification can contain non-functional elements as well as functions; topics such as reliability, usability and performance are examples. These need to be systematically tested as well.

What we need, then, are techniques that can explore the specified behaviour systematically and thoroughly in a way that is as efficient as we can make it. In addition, we use what we know about software to 'home in' on problems; each of the test case design techniques is based on some simple principles that arise from what we know in general about software behaviour.

You need to know five specification-based techniques for the Foundation Certificate:

- Equivalence partitioning
- Boundary value analysis
- Decision table testing
- State transition testing
- Use case testing

You should be capable of generating test cases for the first four of these techniques.

CHECK OF UNDERSTANDING

(1) What do we call the category of test case design techniques that requires knowledge of how the system under test actually works?

(2) What do black-box techniques derive their test cases from?

(3) How do we make specification-based testing work when there is no specification?

Equivalence partitioning

Input partitions

Equivalence partitioning is based on a very simple idea: it is that in many cases the inputs to a program can be 'chunked' into groups of similar inputs. For example, a program that accepts integer values can accept as valid any input that is an integer (i.e. a whole number) and should reject anything else (such as a real number or a character). The range of integers is infinite, though the computer will limit this to some finite value in both the negative and positive directions (simply because it can only handle numbers of a certain size; it is a finite machine). Let us suppose, for the sake of an example, that the program accepts any value between −10,000 and +10,000 (computers actually represent numbers in binary form, which makes the numbers look much less like the ones we are familiar with, but we will stick to a familiar representation). If we imagine a program that separates numbers into two groups according to whether they are positive or negative the total range of integers could be split into three 'partitions': the values that are less than zero; zero; and the values that are greater than zero. Each of these is known as an 'equivalence partition' because every value inside the partition is exactly equivalent to any other value as far as our program is concerned. So if the computer accepts −2,905 as a valid negative integer we would expect it also to accept −3. Similarly, if it accepts 100 it should also accept 2,345 as a positive integer. Note that we are treating zero as a special case. We could, if we chose to, include zero with the positive integers, but my rudimentary specification did not specify that clearly, so it is really left as an undefined value (and it is not untypical to find such ambiguities or undefined areas in specifications). It often suits us to treat zero as a special case for testing where ranges of numbers are involved; we treat it as an equivalence partition with only one member. So we have three valid equivalence partitions in this case.

The equivalence partitioning technique takes advantage of the properties of equivalence partitions to reduce the number of test cases we need to write. Since all the values in an equivalence partition are handled in exactly the same way by a given program, we need only test one of them as a representative of the partition. In the example given, then, we need any positive integer, any negative integer and zero. We generally select values somewhere near the middle of each partition, so we might choose, say, −5,000, 0 and 5,000 as our representatives. These three test inputs would exercise all three partitions and the theory tells us that if the program treats these three values correctly it is very likely to treat all of the other values, all 19,998 of them in this case, correctly.

The partitions we have identified so far are called valid equivalence partitions because they partition the collection of valid inputs, but there are other possible inputs to this program that would not be valid – real numbers, for example. We also have two input partitions of integers that are not valid: integers less than −10,000 and integers greater than 10,000. We should test that the program does not accept these, which is just as important as the program accepting valid inputs.

Non-valid partitions are also important to test. If you think about the example we have been using you will soon recognize that there are far more possible non-valid inputs than valid ones, since all the real numbers (e.g. numbers containing decimals) and all characters are non-valid in this case. It is generally the case that there are far more ways to provide incorrect input than there are to provide correct input; as a result we need to ensure that we have tested the program against the possible non-valid inputs. Here again equivalence partitioning comes to our aid: all real numbers are equally non-valid, as are all alphabetic characters. These represent two non-valid partitions that we should test, using values such as 9.45 and 'r' respectively. There will be many other possible non-valid input partitions, so we may have to limit the test cases to the ones that are most likely to crop up in a real situation.

EXAMPLE EQUIVALENCE PARTITIONS

- Valid input: integers in the range 100 to 999.
    + Valid partition: 100 to 999 inclusive.
    + Non-valid partitions: less than 100, more than 999, real (decimal) numbers and non-numeric characters.
- Valid input: names with up to 20 alphabetic characters.
    + Valid partition: strings of up to 20 alphabetic characters.
    + Non-valid partitions: strings of more than 20 alphabetic characters, strings containing non-alphabetic characters.

Exercise 4.1

Suppose you have a bank account that offers variable interest rates: 0.5 per cent for the first £1,000 credit; 1 per cent for the next £1,000; 1.5 per cent for the rest. If you wanted to check that the bank was handling your account correctly what valid input partitions might you use?

The answer can be found at the end of the chapter.

Output partitions

Just as the input to a program can be partitioned, so can the output. The program in the exercise above could produce outputs of 0.5 per cent, 1 per cent and 1.5 per cent, so we could use test cases that generate each of these outputs as an alternative to generating input partitions. An input value in the range £0.00–£1,000.00 would generate the 0.5 per cent output; a value in the range £1,001.00–£2,000.00 would generate the 1 per cent output; a value greater than £2,000.00 would generate the 1.5 per cent output.

Other partitions

If we know enough about an application we may be able to partition other values instead of or as well as input and output. For example, if a program handles input requests by placing them on one of a number of queues we could, in principle, check that requests end up on the right queue. In this case a stream of inputs can be partitioned according to the queue we anticipate it will be placed into. This is more technical and difficult than input or output partitioning but it is an option that can be considered when appropriate.

PARTITIONS – EXAMPLE 4.1

A mail order company charges £2.95 postage for deliveries if the package weighs less than 2 kg, £3.95 if the package weighs 2 kg or more but less than 5 kg, and £5 for packages weighing 5 kg or more. Generate a set of valid test cases using equivalence partitioning.

The valid input partitions are: under 2 kg; 2 kg or over but less than 5 kg; and 5 kg or over.

Input values could be 1 kg, 3.5 kg, 7.5 kg. These would produce expected results of £2.95, £3.95 and £5 respectively.

In this case there are no non-valid inputs (unless the scales fail).

Exercise 4.2

A mail-order company selling flower seeds charges £3.95 for postage and packing on all orders up to £20 value and £4.95 for orders above £20 value and up to £40 value. For orders above £40 value there is no charge for postage and packing.

If you were using equivalence partitioning to prepare test cases for the postage and packing charges what valid partitions would you define?

What about non-valid partitions?

The answer can be found at the end of the chapter.

Boundary value analysis

One thing we know about the kinds of mistakes that programmers make is that errors tend to cluster around boundaries. For example, if a program should accept a sequence of numbers between 1 and 10, the most likely fault will be that values just outside this range are incorrectly accepted or that values just inside the range are incorrectly rejected. In the programming world these faults coincide with particular programming structures such as the number of times a program loop is executed or the exact point at which a loop should stop executing.

This works well with our equivalence partitioning idea because partitions must have boundaries. A partition of integers between 1 and 99, for instance, has a lowest value, 1, and a highest value, 99. These are called boundary values. Actually they are called valid boundary values because they are the boundaries on the inside of a valid partition. What about the values on the outside? Yes, they have boundaries too. So the boundary of the non-valid values at the lower end will be zero because it is the first value you come to when you step outside the partition at the bottom end. (You can also think of this as the highest value inside the non-valid partition of integers that are less than one, of course.) At the top end of the range we also have a non-valid boundary value, 100.

This is the boundary value technique, more or less. In fact we include one more value when we use boundary value analysis: the rule is that we use the boundary value itself and one value (as close as you can get) either side of the boundary.

So, in this case lower boundary values will be 0, 1, 2 and upper boundary values will be 98, 99, 100. What does 'as close as we can get' mean? It means take the next value in sequence using the precision that has been applied to the partition. If the numbers are to a precision of 0.01, for example, the lower boundary values would be 0.99, 1.00, 1.01 and the upper boundary values would be 98.99, 99.00. 99.01.

The best way to consolidate the idea of boundaries is to look at some examples.

BOUNDARY VALUES – EXAMPLE 4.2

- The boiling point of water – the boundary is at 100 degrees Celsius, so the boundary values will be 99 degrees, 100 degrees, 101 degrees – unless you have a very accurate digital thermometer, in which case they could be 99.9 degrees, 100.0 degrees, 100.1 degrees.

- Exam pass – if an exam has a pass boundary at 40 per cent, merit at 60 per cent and distinction at 80 per cent the boundaries would be 39, 40, 41 for pass, 59, 60, 61 for merit, 79, 80, 81 for distinction. It is unlikely that marks would be recorded at any greater precision than whole numbers.

Exercise 4.3

A system is designed to accept scores from independent markers who have marked the same examination script. Each script should have 5 individual marks, each of which is out of 20, and a total for the script. Two markers' scores are compared and differences greater than three in any question score or 10 overall are flagged for further examination.

Using equivalence partitioning and boundary value analysis identify the boundary values that you would explore for this scenario.

(In practice, some of the boundary values might actually be in other equivalence partitions, and we do not need to test them twice, so the total number of boundary values requiring testing might be less than you might expect.)

The answer can be found at the end of the chapter.

CHECK OF UNDERSTANDING

(1) What is the relationship between a partition and a boundary?

(2) Why are equivalence partitioning and boundary value analysis often used together?

(3) Explain what is meant by 'as close as possible to a boundary'?

Decision table testing

Specifications often contain business rules to define the functions of the system and the conditions under which each function operates. Individual decisions are usually simple, but the overall effect of these logical conditions can become quite complex. As testers we need to be able to assure ourselves that every combination of these conditions that might occur has been tested, so we need to capture all the decisions in a way that enables us to explore their combinations. The mechanism usually used to capture the logical decisions is called a decision table.

A decision table lists all the input conditions that can occur and all the actions that can arise from them. These are structured into a table as rows, with the conditions at the top of the table and the possible actions at the bottom. Business rules, which involve combinations of conditions to produce some combination of actions, are arranged across the top. Each column therefore represents a single business rule (or just 'rule') and shows how input conditions combine to produce actions. Thus each column represents a possible test case, since it identifies both inputs and expected outputs. This is shown schematically in the box below.

DECISION TABLE STRUCTURE

	Business rule 1	Business rule 2	Business rule 3
Condition 1	T	F	T
Condition 2	T	T	T
Condition 3	T	–	F
Action 1	Y	N	Y
Action 2	N	Y	Y

Business rule 1 requires all conditions to be true to generate action 1. Business rule 2 results in action 2 if condition 1 is false and condition 2 is true but does not depend on condition 3. Business rule 3 requires conditions 1 and 2 to be true and condition 3 to be false.

In reality the number of conditions and actions can be quite large, but usually the number of combinations producing specific actions is relatively small. For this reason we do not enter every possible combination of conditions into our decision table, but restrict it to those combinations that correspond to business rules – this is called a limited entry decision table to distinguish it from a decision table with all combinations of inputs identified. In this chapter we will always mean the limited entry kind when we refer to a decision table.

As usual, we use an example to clarify what we mean.

DECISION TESTING – EXAMPLE 4.3

A supermarket has a loyalty scheme that is offered to all customers. Loyalty card holders enjoy the benefits of either additional discounts on all purchases (rule 3) or the acquisition of loyalty points (rule 4), which can be converted into vouchers for the supermarket or to equivalent points in schemes run by partners. Customers without a loyalty card receive an additional discount only if they spend more than £100 on any one visit to the store (rule 2), otherwise only the special offers offered to all customers apply (rule 1).

	Rule 1	Rule 2	Rule 3	Rule 4
Conditions:				
Customer without loyalty card	T	T	F	F
Customer with loyalty card	F	F	T	T
Extra discount selected	–	–	T	F
Spend > £100	F	T	–	–
Actions:				
No discount	T	F	F	F
Extra discount	F	T	T	F
Loyalty points	F	F	F	T

From the decision table we can determine test cases by setting values for the conditions and determining the expected output, e.g. from rule 1 we could input a normal customer with a £50 transaction and check that no discount was applied. The same customer with a £150 transaction (rule 2) should attract a discount. Thus we can see that each column of the decision table represents a possible test case.

CHECK OF UNDERSTANDING

(1) What is a decision table derived from?

(2) Why does decision table testing use limited entry decision tables?

(3) Describe how test cases are identified from decision tables.

(4) Which element of a decision table defines the expected output for a test case?

Exercise 4.4

A mutual insurance company has decided to float its shares on the stock exchange and is offering its members rewards for their past custom at the time of flotation. Anyone with a current policy will benefit provided it is a 'with-profits' policy and they have held it since 2001. Those who meet these criteria can opt for either a cash payment or an allocation of shares in the new company; those who have held a qualifying policy for less than the required time will be eligible for a cash payment but not for shares. Here is a decision table reflecting those rules.

	Rule 1	Rule 2	Rule 3	Rule 4
Conditions:				
Current policy holder	Y	Y	Y	N
Policy holder since 2001	N	Y	N	–
'With-profits' policy	Y	Y	N	–
Actions:				
Eligible for cash payment	Y	Y	N	N
Eligible for share allocations	N	Y	N	N

What expected result would you expect to get for the following test case?

Billy Bunter is a current policy holder who has held a 'with-profits' policy since 2003.

The answer can be found at the end of the chapter.

State transition testing

The previous technique, decision table testing, is particularly useful in systems where combinations of input conditions produce various actions. Now we consider a similar technique, but this time we are concerned with systems in which outputs are triggered by changes to the input conditions, or changes of 'state'; in other words, behaviour depends on current state and past state, and it is the transitions that trigger system behaviour. It will be no surprise to learn that this technique is known as state transition testing or that the main diagram used in the technique is called a state transition diagram.

Look at the box to see an example of a state transition diagram.

STATE TRANSITION DIAGRAMS

A state transition diagram is a representation of the behaviour of a system. It is made up from just two symbols.

The first is

which is the symbol for a state. A state is just what it says it is: the system is 'static', in a stable condition from which it will only change if it is stimulated by an event of some kind. For example, a TV stays 'on' unless you turn it 'off'; a multifunction watch tells the time unless you change mode.

The second is

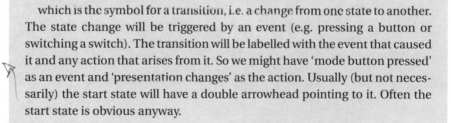

which is the symbol for a transition, i.e. a change from one state to another. The state change will be triggered by an event (e.g. pressing a button or switching a switch). The transition will be labelled with the event that caused it and any action that arises from it. So we might have 'mode button pressed' as an event and 'presentation changes' as the action. Usually (but not necessarily) the start state will have a double arrowhead pointing to it. Often the start state is obvious anyway.

If we have a state transition diagram representation of a system we can analyse the behaviour in terms of what happens when a transition occurs.

Transitions are caused by events and they may generate outputs and/or changes of state. An event is anything that acts as a trigger for a change; it could be an input to the system, or it could be something inside the system that changes for some reason, such as a database field being updated.

In some cases an event generates an output, in others the event changes the system's internal state without generating an output, and in still others an event may cause an output and a change of state. What happens for each change is always deducible from the state transition diagram.

STATE TRANSITION DIAGRAM – EXAMPLE 4.4

A hill-walker's watch has two modes: Time and Altimeter. In Time mode, pressing the Mode switch causes the watch to switch to Alt mode; pressing Alt again returns to Time mode. While the watch is in Alt mode the Set button has no effect.

When the watch is in Time mode pressing the Set button transitions the watch into Set Hrs, from which the Hrs display can be incremented by pressing the Set button. If the Mode switch is pressed while the watch is in Set Hrs mode the watch transitions to Set Mins mode, in which pressing the Set button increments the Mins display. If the Mode button is pressed in this mode the watch transitions back to Time mode (Figure 4.1).

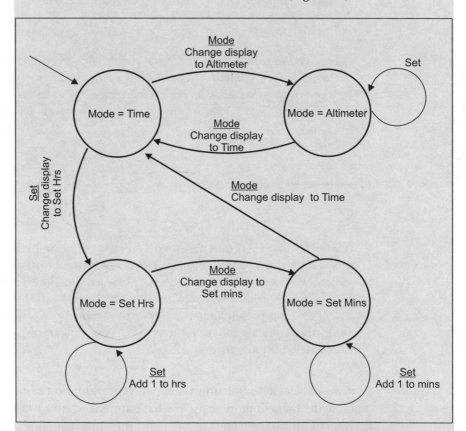

FIGURE 4.1   *State transition diagram of the hill-walker's watch*

Note that not all events have an effect in all states. Where an event does not have an effect on a given state it is usually omitted, but it can be shown as an arrow starting from the state and returning to the same state to indicate that no transition takes place; this is sometimes known as a 'null' transition or an 'invalid' transition.

Rather than work out what happens for each event each time we want to initiate a test, we can take the intermediate step of creating what is known as a state table (ST). An ST records all the possible events and all the possible states; for each combination of event and state it shows the outcome in terms of the new state and any outputs that are generated.

The ST is the source from which we usually derive test cases. It makes sense to do it this way because the analysis of state transitions takes time and can be a source of errors; it is better to do this task once and then have a simple way of generating tests from it than to do it every time we want to generate a new test case.

Here is an example of what an ST looks like.

STATE TABLE – EXAMPLE 4.4

An ST has a row for each state in the state transition diagram and a column for every event. For a given row and column intersection we read off the state from the state transition diagram and note what effect (if any) each event has. If the event has no effect we label the table entry with a symbol that indicates that nothing happens; this is sometimes called a 'null' transition or an 'invalid' transition. If the event does have an effect we label the table entry with the state to which the system transitions when the given event occurs; if there is also an output (there is sometimes but not always) the output is indicated in the same table entry separated from the new state by the '/' symbol. The example shown in Table 4.1 is the ST for Figure 4.1, which we drew in the previous box.

TABLE 4.1 *ST for the hill-walker's watch*

	Mode	**Alt**	**Set**
Mode = Time	N	Mode = Altimeter/Change Display to Altimeter	Set Hrs
Mode = Altimeter	N	Mode = Time/Change Display to Time	N
Set Hrs	Set Mins/Change display to Mins	N	Set Hrs/Add 1 to Hrs
Set Mins	Mode = Time/Change Display to Time	N	Set Mins/Add 1 to Mins

Once we have an ST it is a simple exercise to generate the test cases that we need to exercise the functionality by triggering state changes.

STATE TRANSITION TESTING – EXAMPLE 4.4

We generate test cases by stepping through the ST. If we begin in Time mode then the first test case might be to press Mode and observe that the watch changes to Alt state; pressing Mode again becomes test case 2, which returns the watch to Time state. Test case 3 could press Set and observe the change to Set Hrs mode and then try a number of presses of Set to check that the incrementing mechanism works. In this way we can work our way systematically round the ST until every single transition has been exercised. If we want to be more sophisticated we can exercise pairs of transitions, e.g. pressing Set twice as a single test case, to check that Hrs increments correctly. We should also test all the negative cases, i.e. those cases where the ST indicates there is no valid transition.

CHECK OF UNDERSTANDING

(1) What is the main use of an ST for testers?

(2) Name three components of a state transition diagram.

(3) How are negative tests identified from an ST?

(4) What is meant by the term 'invalid transition'?

Exercise 4.5

In the state transition diagram in Figure 4.2, which of the sequences of transitions below would be valid?

a.   ABCDE
b.   FEABC
c.   ABCEF
d.   EFADC

The answer can be found at the end of the chapter.

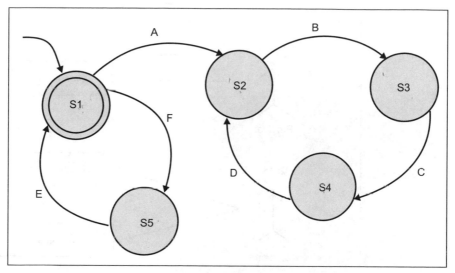

FIGURE 4.2   *State transition diagram*

Use case testing

Use cases are one way of specifying functionality as business scenarios or process flows. They capture the individual interactions between ' actors' and the system. An actor represents a particular type of user and the use cases capture the interactions that each user takes part in to produce some output that is of value. Test cases based on use cases, often called scenarios, are therefore particularly useful in exercising business rules or process flows and will often identify gaps or weaknesses in these that would not be found by exercising individual components in isolation.

In practice, writing a test case to represent each use case is a good starting point for testing.

LIVERPOOL JOHN MOORES UNIVERSITY
LEARNING SERVICES

USE CASES

In a use case diagram (e.g. Figure 4.3) each type of user is known as an actor, and an actor stands for all users of the type. Use cases are activities carried out for that actor by the system. This is, in effect, a high-level view of requirements.

The diagram alone does not provide enough detail for testing, so we need some textual description of the processes involved as well.

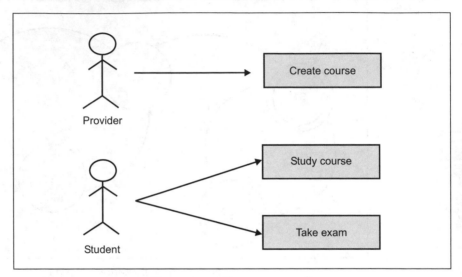

FIGURE 4.3 *Use case example*

 Use case testing has the major benefit that it relates to real user processes, so it offers an opportunity to exercise a complete process flow. The principles applied elsewhere can be applied here: first test the highest priority (highest value) use cases by taking typical examples; then exercise some attempts at incorrect process flows; and then exercise the boundaries.

CHECK OF UNDERSTANDING

(1) What is the purpose of a use case?

(2) What is the relationship between a use case and a test case?

(3) Briefly compare equivalence partitioning and use case testing.

STRUCTURE-BASED OR WHITE-BOX TECHNIQUES

Structure-based test techniques are used to explore program structures. Instead of exercising the code to see if it functions correctly they focus on ensuring that particular elements of the code itself are exercised. For example, we can use structural testing techniques to ensure that each statement in the code is executed at least once. Structure-based techniques involve generating test cases from code, so we need to be able to read and analyse code. As you will see later, in Chapter 6, code analysis and structure-based testing are mostly done by specialist tools in reality, but a knowledge of the techniques is still valuable. You may wish to run simple test cases on code to ensure that it is basically sound before you begin detailed functional testing, or you may want to interpret test results from programmers to ensure that their testing adequately exercises the code.

Our starting point, then, is the code itself.

READING AND INTERPRETING CODE

In a Foundation-level examination the term 'code' will always mean pseudo code. Pseudo code is a much more limited language than any real programming language but it enables designers to create all the main control structures needed by programs. It is sometimes used to document designs before they are coded into a programming language.

In the next few boxes we will introduce all the essential elements of pseudo code that you will need to be able to analyse code and create test cases for the Foundation examination.

Wherever you see the word 'code' from here on in this chapter read it as 'pseudo code'.

Real programming languages have a wide variety of forms and structures – so many that we could not adequately cover them all. The advantage of pseudo code in this respect is that it has a simple structure.

OVERALL PROGRAM STRUCTURE

Code can be of two types, executable and non-executable. Executable code instructs the computer to take some action; non-executable code is used to prepare the computer to do its calculations but it does not involve any actions. For example, reserving space to store a calculation (this is called a declaration statement) involves no actions. In pseudo code non-executable statements will be at the beginning of the program; the start of the executable part is usually identified by BEGIN, and the end of the program by END. So we get the following structure:

```
1    Non-executable statements
2    BEGIN
3
4    Executable statements
5
6    END
```

If we were counting executable statements we would count lines 2, 4 and 6. Line 1 is not counted because it is non-executable. Lines 3 and 5 are ignored because they are blank.

If there are no non-executable statements there may be no BEGIN or END either, but there will always be something separating non-executable from executable statements where both are present.

Now we have a picture of an overall program structure we can look inside the code. Surprisingly, there are only three ways that executable code can be structured, so we only have three structures to learn. The first is simple and is known as sequence: that just means that the statements are exercised one after the other as they appear on the page. The second structure is called selection: in this case the computer has to decide if a condition (known as a Boolean condition) is true or false. If it is true the computer takes one route, and if it is false the computer takes a different route. Selection structures therefore involve decisions. The third structure is called iteration; it simply involves the computer exercising a chunk of code more than once; the number of times it exercises the chunk of code depends on the value of a condition (just as in the selection case). Let us look at that a little closer.

PROGRAMMING STRUCTURES

SEQUENCE

The following program is purely sequential:

```
1    Read A
2    Read B
3    C = A + B
```

The BEGIN and END have been omitted in this case since there were no non-executable statements; this is not strictly correct but is common practice, so it is wise to be aware of it and remember to check whether there are any non-executable statements when you do see BEGIN and END in a program. The computer would execute those three statements in sequence, so it would read (input) a value into A (this is just a name for a storage location), then read another value into B, and finally add them together and put the answer into C.

SELECTION

```
1    IF P > 3
2    THEN
3        X = X + Y
4    ELSE
5        X = X - Y
6    ENDIF
```

Here we ask the computer to evaluate the condition P > 3, which means compare the value that is in location P with 3. If the value in P is greater than 3 then the condition is true; if not, the condition is false. The computer then selects which statement to execute next. If the condition is true it will execute the part labelled THEN, so it executes line 3. Similarly if the condition is false it will execute line 5. After it has executed either line 3 or line 5 it will go to line 6, which is the end of the selection (IF THEN ELSE) structure. From there it will continue with the next line in sequence.

There may not always be an ELSE part, as below:

```
1    IF P > 3
2    THEN
3        X = X + Y
4    ENDIF
```

In this case the computer executes line 3 if the condition is true, or moves on to line 4 (the next line in sequence) if the condition is false.

ITERATION

Iteration structures are called loops. The most common loop is known as a DO WHILE (or WHILE DO) loop and is illustrated below:

```
1    X = 15
2    Count = 0
3    WHILE X < 20 DO
4        X = X + 1
5        Count = Count + 1
6    END DO
```

As with the selection structures there is a decision. In this case the condition that is tested at the decision is X < 20. If the condition is true the program 'enters the loop' by executing the code between DO and END DO. In this case the value of X is increased by one and the value of Count is increased by one. When this is done the program goes back to line 3 and repeats the test. If X < 20 is still true the program 'enters the loop' again. This continues as long as the condition is true. If the condition is false the program goes directly to line 6 and then continues to the next sequential instruction. In the program fragment above the loop will be executed five times before the value of X reaches 20 and causes the loop to terminate. The value of Count will then be 5.

There is another variation of the loop structure known as a REPEAT UNTIL loop. It looks like this:

```
1    X = 15
2    Count = 0
3    REPEAT
4        X = X + 1
5          Count = Count + 1
6    UNTIL X = 20
```

The difference from a DO WHILE loop is that the condition is at the end, so the loop will always be executed at least once. Every time the code inside the loop is executed the program checks the condition. When the condition is true the program continues with the next sequential instruction. The outcome of this REPEAT UNTIL loop will be exactly the same as the DO WHILE loop above.

CHECK OF UNDERSTANDING

(1) What is meant by the term executable statement?

(2) Briefly describe the two forms of looping structure introduced in this section.

(3) What is a selection structure?

(4) How many different paths are there through a selection structure?

Flow charts

Now that we can read code we can go a step further and create a visual representation of the structure which is much easier to work with. The simplest visual structure to draw is the flow chart, which has only two symbols. Rectangles represent sequential statements and diamonds represent decisions. More than one sequential statement can be placed inside a single rectangle as long as there are no decisions in the sequence. Any decision is represented by a diamond, including those associated with loops.

Let us look at our earlier examples again.

To create a flow chart representation of a complete program (see Example 4.5) all we need to do is to connect together all the different bits of structure.

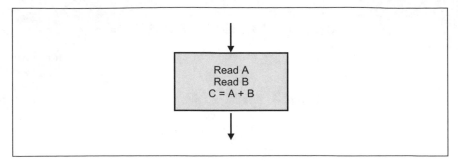

FIGURE 4.4   *Flow chart for a sequential program*

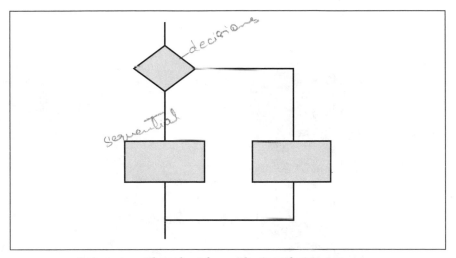

FIGURE 4.5   *Flow chart for a selection (decision) structure*

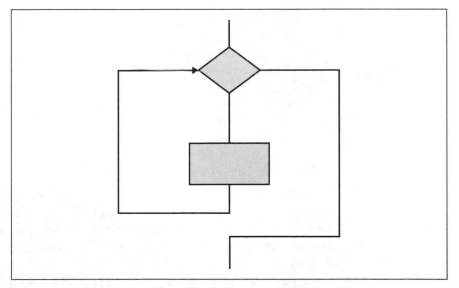

FIGURE 4.6   *Flow chart for an iteration (loop) structure*

PROGRAM ANALYSIS – EXAMPLE 4.5

Here is a simple program for calculating the mean and maximum of three integers.

```
1    Program MaxandMean
2
3    A, B, C, Maximum: type Integer
4    Mean: type Real
5
6    Begin
7
8    Read A
9    Read B
10   Read C
11   Mean = (A + B + C)/3
12
13   If A > B
14   Then
15       If A > C
16       Then
17           Maximum = A
18       Else
19           Maximum = C
20       Endif
21   Else
22       If B > C
23       Then
24           Maximum = B
25       Else
26           Maximum = C
27       Endif
28   Endif
29
30   Print ("Mean of A, B and C is ", Mean)
31   Print ("Maximum of A, B, C is ", Maximum)
32
33   End
```

Note one important thing about this code: it has some non-executable statements (those before the **Begin** and those after the **Begin** that are actually blank lines) that we will have to take account of when we come to count the number of executable statements later. The line numbering makes it a little easier to do the counting.

By the way, you may have noticed that the program does not recognize if two of the numbers are the same value, but simplicity is more important than sophistication at this stage.

This program can be expressed as a flow chart; have a go at drawing it before you look at the solution in the text.

Figure 4.7 shows the flow chart for Example 4.5.

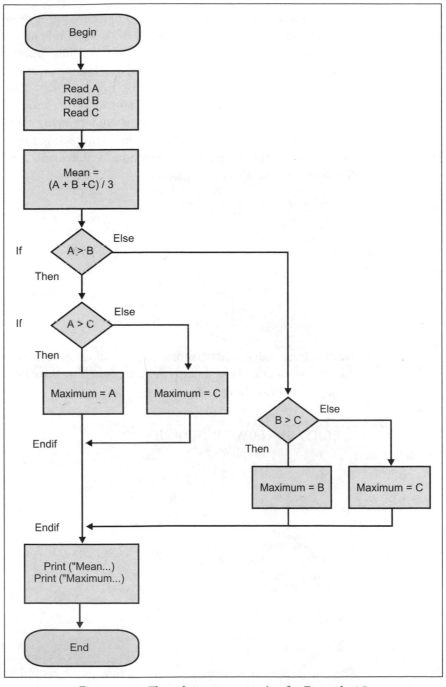

FIGURE 4.7   *Flow chart representation for Example 4.5*

Before we move on to look at how we generate test cases for code, we need to look briefly at another form of graphical representation called the control flow graph.

Control flow graphs

A control flow graph provides a method of representing the decision points and the flow of control within a piece of code, so it is just like a flow chart except that it only shows decisions. A control flow graph is produced by looking only at the statements affecting the flow of control.

The graph itself is made up of two symbols: nodes and edges. A node represents any point where the flow of control can be modified (i.e. decision points), or the points where a control structure returns to the main flow (e.g. END WHILE or ENDIF). An edge is a line connecting any two nodes. The closed area contained within a collection of nodes and edges, as shown in the diagram, is known as a region.

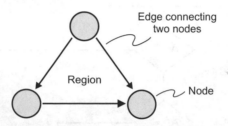

We can draw 'subgraphs' to represent individual structures. For a flow graph the representation of sequence is just a straight line, since there is no decision to cause any branching.

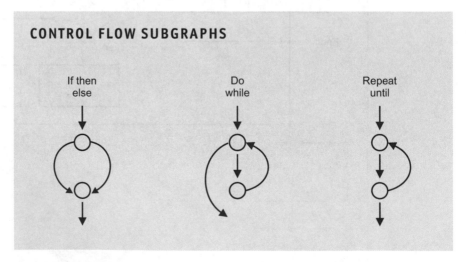

The subgraphs show what the control flow graph would look like for the program structures we are already familiar with.

DRAWING A CONTROL FLOW GRAPH

The steps are as follows:

(1) Analyse the component to identify all control structures, i.e. all statements that can modify the fkow of control, ignoring all sequential statements.

(2) Add a node for any decision statement.

(3) Expand the node by substituting the appropriate subgraph representing the structure at the decision point.

Any chunk of code can be represented by using these subgraphs.

As an example, we will return to Example 4.5.

Step 1 breaks the code into statements and identifies the control structures, ignoring the sequential statements, in order to identify the decision points; these are highlighted below.

```
1    Program MaxandMean
2
3    A, B, C, Maximum: type Integer
4    Mean: type Real
5
6    Begin
7
8    Read A
9    Read B
10   Read C
11   Mean = (A + B + C)/3
12
13   If A > B
14   Then
15       If A > C
16       Then
17           Maximum = A
18       Else
19           Maximum = C
20       Endif
21   Else
22       If B > C
23       Then
24           Maximum = B
25       Else
26           Maximum = C
27       Endif
28   Endif
```

```
29
30   Print ("Mean of A, B and C is ", Mean)
31   Print ("Maximum of A, B, C is ", Maximum)
32
33   End
```

Step 2 adds a node for each branching or decision statement (Figure 4.8).

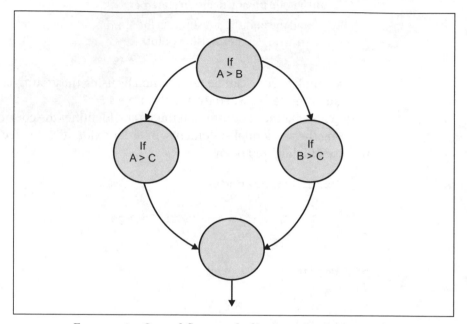

FIGURE 4.8   *Control flow graph showing subgraphs as nodes*

Step 3 expands the nodes by substituting the appropriate subgraphs (Figure 4.9).

CHECK OF UNDERSTANDING

(1) What is the difference between a flow chart and a control flow graph?

(2) Name the three fundamental program structures that can be found in programs.

(3) Briefly explain what is meant by an edge, a node and a region in a control flow graph.

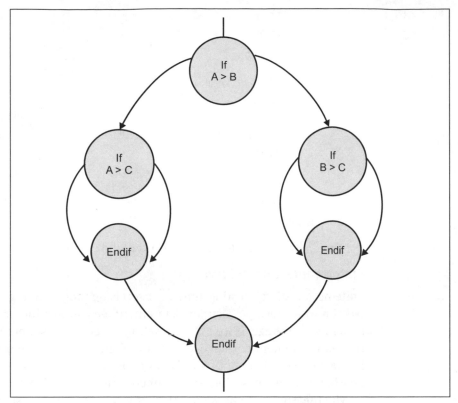

FIGURE 4.9 *Control flow graph with subgraphs expanded*

Exercise 4.6

Draw a flow chart and a control flow graph to represent the following code:

```
1    Program OddandEven
2
3    A, B: Real;
4    Odd: Integer;
5
6    Begin
7        Read A
8        Read B
9        C = A + B
10       D = A - B
11       Odd = 0
12
13       If A/2 DIV 2 <> 0 (DIV gives the remainder after division)
14       Then Odd = Odd + 1
15       Endif
16
```

```
17      If B/2 DIV 2 <> 0
18      Then Odd = Odd + 1
19      Endif
20
21      If Odd = 1
22      Then
23          Print ("C is odd")
24          Print ("D is odd")
25      Else
26          Print ("C is even")
27          Print ("D is even")
28      Endif
29  End
```

The answer can be found at the end of the chapter.

Statement testing and coverage

Statement testing is testing aimed at exercising programming statements. If we aim to test every executable statement we call this full or 100 per cent statement coverage. If we exercise half the executable statements this is 50 per cent statement coverage, and so on. Remember: we are only interested in executable statements, so we do not count non-executable statements at all when we are measuring statement coverage.

Why measure statement coverage? It is a very basic measure that testing has been (relatively) thorough. After all, a suite of tests that had not exercised all of the code would not be considered complete. Actually, achieving 100 per cent statement coverage does not tell us very much, and there are much more rigorous coverage measures that we can apply, but it provides a baseline from which we can move on to more useful coverage measures. Look at the following pseudo code:

```
1   Program Coverage Example
2   A, X: type Integer
3   Begin
4       Read A
5       Read X
6       If A > 1 AND X = 2
7       Then
8           X=X/A
9       Endif
10      If A = 2 OR X = 2
11      Then
12          X = X + 1
13      Endif
14  End
```

A flow chart can represent this, as in Figure 4.10.

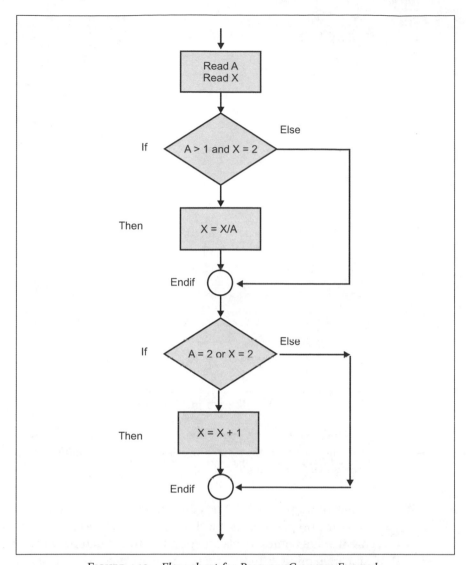

FIGURE 4.10   *Flow chart for Program Coverage Example*

Having explored flow charts and flow graphs a little, you will see that flow charts are very good at showing you where the executable statements are; they are all represented by diamonds or rectangles and where there is no rectangle there is no executable code. A flow graph is less cluttered, showing only the structural details, in particular where the program branches and rejoins. Do we need both diagrams? Well, neither has everything that we need. However, we can produce a version of the flow graph that allows us to determine statement coverage.

To do this we build a conventional control flow graph but then we add a node for every branch in which there is one or more statements. Take the Program Coverage example; we can produce its flow graph easily as shown in Figure 4.11.

THE HYBRID FLOW GRAPH

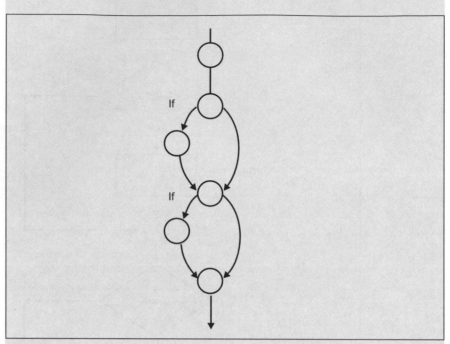

FIGURE 4.11 *The hybrid flow graph*

Note the additional nodes that represent the edges with executable statements in them; they make it a little easier to identify what needs to be counted for statement coverage.

Before we proceed, let us confirm what happens when a program runs. Once the program starts it will run through to the end executing every statement that it comes to in sequence. Control structures will be the only diversion from this end-to-end sequence, so we need to understand what happens with the control structures when the program runs. The best way to do that is to 'dry run' the program with some inputs; this means writing down the inputs and then stepping through the program logic noting what happens at each step and what values change. When you get to the end you will know what the output values (if any) will be and you will know exactly what path the program has taken through the logic.

PATHS THROUGH A PROGRAM

Flow charts, control flow graphs and hybrid flow graphs all show essentially the same information, but sometimes one format is more helpful than another. We have identified the hybrid flow graph as a useful combination of the control flow graph and the control flow chart. To make it even more useful we can add to it labels to indicate the paths that a program can follow through the code. All we need to do is to label each edge; paths are then made up from sequences of the labels, such as abeh, which make up a path through the code (see Figure 4.12).

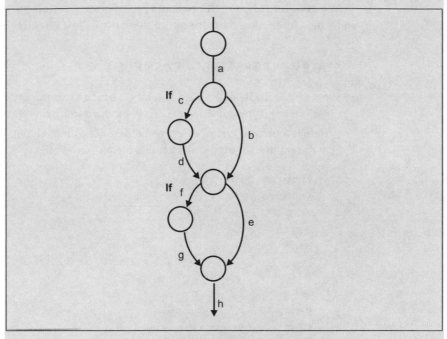

FIGURE 4.12 *Paths through the hybrid flow graph*

In the Program Coverage example, for which we drew the flow chart in Figure 4.10, 100 per cent statement coverage can be achieved by writing a single test case that follows the path acdfgh (using lower case letters to label the arcs on the diagram that represent path fragments). By setting A = 2 and X = 2 at point a, every statement will be executed once. However, what if the first decision should be an OR rather than an AND? The test would not have detected the error, since the condition will be true in both cases. Similarly, if the second decision should have stated X > 2 this error would have gone undetected because the value of A guarantees that the condition is true. Also, there is a path through the program in which X goes unchanged (the path abeh). If this were an error it would also go undetected.

Remember that statement coverage takes into account only executable statements. There are 12 in the Program Coverage example if we count the **BEGIN** and **END** statements, so statement coverage would be 12/12 or 100 per cent. There are alternative ways to count executable statements: some people count the **BEGIN** and **END** statements; some count the lines containing **IF**, **THEN** and **ELSE**; some count none of these. It does not matter as long as:

- You exclude the non-executable statements that precede **BEGIN**.
- You ignore blank lines that have been inserted for clarity.
- You are consistent about what you do or do not include in the count with respect to control structures.

As a general rule, for the reasons given above, statement coverage is too weak to be considered an adequate measure of test effectiveness.

STATEMENT TESTING – EXAMPLE 4.6

Here is an example of the kind you might see in an exam. Try to answer the question, but if you get stuck the answer follows immediately in the text.

Here is a program. How many test cases will you need to achieve 100 per cent statement coverage and what will the test cases be?

```
1    Program BestInterest
2    Interest, Base Rate, Balance: Real
3
4    Begin
5    Base Rate = 0.035
6    Interest = Base Rate
7
8    Read (Balance)
9    If Balance > 1000
10   Then
11       Interest = Interest + 0.005
12       If Balance < 10000
13       Then
14           Interest = Interest + 0.005
15       Else
16           Interest = Interest + 0.010
17       Endif
18   Endif
19
20   Balance = Balance × (1 + Interest)
21
22   End
```

Figure 4.13 shows what the flow graph looks like. It is drawn in the hybrid flow graph format so that you can see which branches need to be exercised for statement coverage.

It is clear from the flow graph that the left-hand side (Balance below £1,000) need not be exercised, but there are two alternative paths (Balance between £1,000 and £10,000 and Balance > £10,000) that need to be exercised.

So we need two test cases for 100 per cent statement coverage and Balance = £5,000, Balance = £20,000 will be suitable test cases.

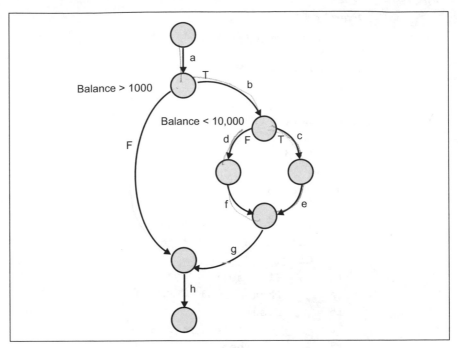

FIGURE 4.13   *Paths through the hybrid flow graph*

Alternatively we can aim to follow the paths abcegh and abdfgh marked on the flow graph. How many test cases do we need to do that?

We can do this with one test case to set the initial balance value to a value between £1,000 and £10,000 (to follow abcegh) and one test case to set the initial balance to something higher than £10,000, say £12,000 (to follow path abdfgh).

So we need two test cases to achieve 100 per cent statement coverage in this case.

CHECK OF UNDERSTANDING

(1) What is meant by statement coverage?

(2) In a flow chart, how do you decide which paths to include in determining how many test cases are needed to achieve a given level of statement coverage?

(3) Does 100 per cent statement coverage exercise all the paths through a program?

Exercise 4.7

For the following program:

```
1    Program Grading
2
3    StudentScore: Integer
4    Result: String
5
6    Begin
7
8    Read StudentScore
9
10   If StudentScore > 79
11   Then Result = "Distinction"
12   Else
13       If Result > 59
14       Then Result = "Merit"
15       Else
16           If Result > 39
17           Then Result = "Pass"
18           Else Result = "Fail"
19           Endif
20       Endif
21   Endif
22   Print ("Your result is", Result)
23   End
```

How many test cases would be needed for 100 per cent statement coverage?

The answer can be found at the end of the chapter.

Decision testing and coverage

Decision testing aims to ensure that the decisions in a program are adequately exercised. Decisions, as you know, are part of selection and iteration structures; we see them in IF THEN ELSE constructs and in DO WHILE or REPEAT UNTIL loops. To test a decision we need to exercise it when the associated condition is true and when the condition is false; this guarantees that both exits from the decision are exercised.

As with statement testing, decision testing has an associated coverage measure and we normally aim to achieve 100 per cent decision coverage. Decision coverage is measured by counting the number of decisions exercised (i.e. both exits are exercised) divided by the total number of decisions in a given program. It is usually expressed as a percentage.

The usual starting point is a control flow graph, from which we can visualize all the possible decisions and their exit paths. Have a look at the following example.

```
1    Program Check
2
3    Count, Sum, Index: Integer
4
5    Begin
6
7    Index = 0
8    Sum = 0
9    Read (Count)
10   Read (New)
11
12   While Index <= Count
13   Do
14       If New < 0
15       Then
16           Sum = Sum + 1
17       Endif
18       Index = Index + 1
19       Read (New)
20   Enddo
21
22   Print ("There were", Sum, "negative numbers in the
     input stream")
23
24   End
```

This program has a WHILE loop in it. There is a golden rule about WHILE loops. If the condition at the WHILE statement is true when the program reaches it for the first time then any test case will exercise that decision in both directions because it will eventually be false when the loop terminates. For example, as long as Index is less than Count when the program reaches the loop for the first time, the condition will be true and the loop will be entered. Each time the program runs through the loop it will increase the value of Index by one, so eventually Index will reach the value of Count and pass it, at which stage the condition is false and the loop will not be entered. So the decision at the start of the loop is exercised through both its true exit and its false exit by a single test case. This makes the assumption that the logic of the loop is sound, but we are assuming that we are receiving this program from the developers who will have debugged it.

Now all we have to do is to make sure that we exercise the **If** statement inside the loop through both its true and false exits. We can do this by ensuring that the input stream has both negative and positive numbers in it.

For example, a test case that sets the variable Count to 5 and then inputs the values 1, 5, −2, −3, 6 will exercise all the decisions fully and provide us with 100 per cent decision coverage. Note that this is considered to be a single test case, even though there is more than one value for the variable New, because the values are all input in a single execution of the program. This example does not provide the smallest set of inputs that would achieve 100 per cent decision coverage, but it does provide a valid example.

Although loops are a little more complicated to understand than programs without loops, they can be easier to test once you get the hang of them.

DECISION TESTING – EXAMPLE 4.7

Let us try an example without a loop now.

```
1    Program Age Check
2
3    CandidateAge: Integer;
4
5    Begin
6
7    Read(CandidateAge)
8
9    If CandidateAge < 18
10   Then
11       Print ("Candidate is too young")
12   Else
13       If CandidateAge > 30
14       Then
15           Print ("Candidate is too old")
16       Else
17           Print("Candidate may join Club 18-30")
18       Endif
19   Endif
20
21   End
```

Have a go at calculating how many test cases are needed for 100 per cent decision coverage and see if you can identify suitable test cases.

Figure 4.14 shows the flow graph drawn in the hybrid flow graph format.

How many test cases will we need to achieve 100 per cent decision coverage? Well each test case will just run through from top to bottom, so we can only exercise one branch of the structure at a time.

We have labelled the path fragments a, b, c, d, e, f, g, h, i, j and you can see that we have three alternative routes through the program – path abhj, path acegij and path acdfij. That needs three test cases.

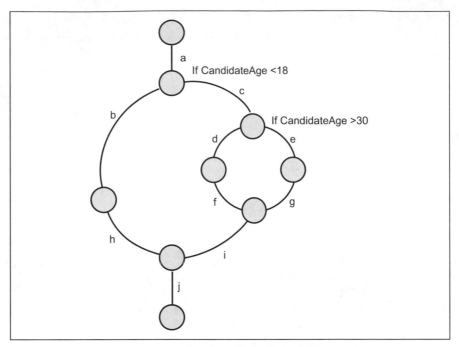

FIGURE 4.14 *Paths through the hybrid flow graph*

The first test case needs decision 1 to be true – so CandidateAge = 16 will be OK here. The second needs to make the first decision false and the second decision true, so CandidateAge must be more than 18 and more than 30 – let us say 40. The third test case needs the first decision to be false and the second decision to be false, so CandidateAge of 21 would do here. (You cannot tell which exit is true and which is false in the second decision; if you want to, you can label the exits T and F, though in this case it does not really matter because we intend to exercise them both anyway.)

So, we need three test cases for 100 per cent decision coverage:

     CandidateAge = 16

     CandidateAge = 21

     CandidateAge = 40

which will exercise all the decisions.

Note that we have exercised the false exit from the first decision, which would not have been necessary for statement coverage, so decision coverage gives us that little bit extra in return for a little more work.

CHECK OF UNDERSTANDING

(1) What is the purpose of decision testing?

(2) How many test cases are needed to exercise a single decision?

(3) How many test cases are needed to exercise a loop structure?

Exercise 4.8

This program reads a list of non-negative numbers terminated by −1.

```
1    Program Counting numbers
2
3    A: Integer
4    Count: Integer
5
6    Begin
7
8    Read A
9    While A <> -1
10   Do
11       Count = Count + 1
12       Read A
13   EndDo
14
15   Print ("There are", Count, "numbers in the list")
16   End
```

How many test cases are needed to achieve 100 per cent decision coverage?

The answer can be found at the end of the chapter.

Other structure-based techniques

More sophisticated techniques are available to provide increasingly complete code coverage. In some applications these are essential: for example, in a safety-critical system it is vital to know that nothing unacceptable happens at any point when the code is executed. Would you like to 'fly by wire' if you did not know what was happening in the software? The many well-documented mishaps in computer-controlled systems provide compelling examples of what can happen if code – even code that is not providing essential functionality in some cases – does something unexpected. Measures such as condition coverage and multiple condition coverage are used to reduce the likelihood that code will behave in unpredictable ways by examining more of it in more complex scenarios.

Coverage is also applicable to other types and levels of structure. For example, at the integration level it is useful to know what percentage of modules or interfaces has been exercised by a test suite, while at the functional level it is helpful to step through all the possible paths of a menu structure. We can also apply the idea of coverage to areas outside the computer, e.g. by exercising all the possible paths through a business process as testing scenarios.

EXPERIENCE-BASED TECHNIQUES

Experience-based techniques are those that you fall back on when there is no adequate specification from which to derive specification-based test cases or no time to run the full structured set of tests. They use the users' and the testers' experience to determine the most important areas of a system and to exercise these areas in ways that are both consistent with expected use (and abuse) and likely to be the sites of errors – this is where the experience comes in. Even when specifications are available it is worth supplementing the structured tests with some that you know by experience have found defects in other similar systems.

Techniques range from the simplistic approach of ad hoc testing or error guessing through to the more sophisticated techniques such as exploratory testing, but all tap the knowledge and experience of the tester rather than systematically exploring a system against a written specification.

Error guessing

Error guessing is a very simple technique that takes advantage of a tester's skill, intuition and experience with similar applications to identify special tests that may not be easy to capture by the more formal techniques. When applied after systematic techniques, error guessing can add another value in identifying and exercising test cases that target known or suspected weaknesses or that simply address aspects of the application that have been found to be problematical in the past.

The main drawback of error guessing is its varying effectiveness, depending as it does on the experience of the tester deploying it. However, if several testers and/or users contribute to constructing a list of possible errors and tests are designed to attack each error listed, this weakness can be effectively overcome. Another way to make error guessing more structured is by the creation of defect and failure lists. These lists can use available defect and failure data (where this exists) as a starting point, but the list can be expanded by using the testers' and users' experience of why the application under test in particular is likely to fail. The defect and failure list can be used as the basis of a set of tests that are applied after the systematic techniques have been used.

Exploratory testing

Exploratory testing is a technique that combines the experience of testers with a structured approach to testing where specifications are either missing or inadequate and where there is severe time pressure. It exploits concurrent test design, test execution, test logging and learning within time-boxes and is structured around a test charter containing test objectives. In this way exploratory testing maximizes the amount of testing that can be achieved within a limited time frame, using test objectives to maintain focus on the most important areas.

SYSTEMATIC AND EXPERIENCE-BASED TECHNIQUES

How do we decide which is the best technique? There are some simple rules of thumb:

(1) Always make functional testing the first priority. It may be necessary to test early code products using structural techniques, but we only really learn about the quality of software when we can see what it does.

(2) When basic functional testing is complete that is a good time to think about test coverage. Have you exercised all the functions, all the requirements, all the code? Coverage measures defined at the beginning as exit criteria can now come into play. Where coverage is inadequate extra tests will be needed.

(3) Use structural methods to supplement functional methods where possible. Even if functional coverage is adequate, it will usually be worth checking statement and decision coverage to ensure that enough of the code has been exercised during testing.

(4) Once systematic testing is complete there is an opportunity to use experience-based techniques to ensure that all the most important and most error-prone areas of the software have been exercised. In some circumstances, such as poor specifications or time pressure, experience-based testing may be the only viable option.

CHOOSING TEST TECHNIQUES

The decision of which test technique to use is not a simple one. There are many factors to bear in mind, some of which are listed in the box.

KEY SELECTION FACTORS

- Type of system
- Regulatory standards
- Customer or contractual requirements
- Level of risk
- Type of risk
- Test objectives
- Documentation available
- Knowledge of the testers
- Time and budget
- Development life cycle
- Use case models
- Experience of type of defects found

One or more of these factors may be important on any given occasion. Some leave no room for selection: regulatory or contractual requirements leave the tester with no choice. Test objectives, where they relate to exit criteria such as test coverage, may also lead to mandatory techniques. Where documentation is not available, or where time and budget are limited, the use of experience-based techniques may be favoured. All others provide pointers within a broad framework: level and type of risk will push the tester towards a particular approach, where high risk is a good reason for using systematic techniques; knowledge of testers, especially where this is limited, may narrow down the available choices; the type of system and the development life cycle will encourage testers to lean in one direction or another depending on their own particular experience. There are few clear-cut cases, and the exercise of sound judgement in selecting appropriate techniques is a mark of a good test manager or team leader.

CHECK OF UNDERSTANDING

(1) What is meant by experience-based testing?

(2) Briefly compare error guessing and exploratory testing.

(3) When is the best time to use experience-based testing?

SUMMARY

In this chapter we have considered the most important terminology needed in discussing the specification stage of the fundamental test process, which was introduced in Chapter 1. We explained how test conditions are derived and how test cases can be designed and grouped into test procedures for execution.

Test design techniques were categorized into three main groups known as specification-based or black-box techniques, structure-based or white-box techniques, and experience-based techniques.

Specification-based techniques introduced were equivalence partitioning, boundary value analysis, state transition testing, decision table testing and use case testing. Specific worked examples of all except use case testing were given (and this was excluded solely because the examination does not require the ability to generate test cases from use cases). Structure-based techniques were introduced and worked examples were given for statement testing and decision testing. Experience-based techniques introduced included error guessing and exploratory testing.

Finally the factors involved in selecting test case design techniques were discussed and guidance given on the selection criteria to be applied.

Example Examination Questions With Answers

E1. K1 question

Which of the following describes structure-based (white-box) test case design techniques?

a.   Test cases are derived systematically from models of the system.
b.   Test cases are derived systematically from the tester's experience.
c.   Test cases are derived systematically from the delivered code.
d.   Test cases are derived from the developers' experience.

E2. K1 question

Which of the following is a structure-based (white-box) technique?

a.   Decision table testing
b.   State transition testing
c.   Statement testing
d.   Boundary value analysis

E3. K3 question

A washing machine has three temperature bands for different kinds of fabrics: fragile fabrics are washed at temperatures between 15 and 30 degrees Celsius; normal fabrics are washed at temperatures between 31 and 60 degrees Celsius; heavily soiled and tough fabrics are washed at temperatures between 61 and 100 degrees Celsius.

Which of the following contains only values that are in **different** equivalence partitions?

a.   15, 30, 60
b.   20, 35, 60
c.   25, 45, 75
d.   12, 35, 55

E4. K3 question

Consider the following pseudo code:

```
1   Begin
2   Read Time
3   If Time < 12 Then
4       Print(Time, "am")
5   Endif
6   If Time > 12 Then
7       Print(Time -12, "pm")
8   Endif
9   End
```

How many test cases are needed to achieve 100 per cent decision coverage?

a. 1
b. 2
c. 3
d. 4

E5. K1 question

What is the main purpose of use case testing?

a. To identify defects in process flows related to typical use of the system.
b. To identify defects in the connections between components.
c. To identify defects in the system related to extreme scenarios.
d. To identify defects in the system related to the use of unapproved programming practices.

E6. K2 question

Which of the following are the **most** important factors to be taken into account when selecting test techniques?

(i) Tools available.
(ii) Regulatory standards.
(iii) Experience of the development team.
(iv) Knowledge of the test team.
(v) The need to maintain levels of capability in each technique

a. (i) and (ii)
b. (ii) and (iv)
c. (iii) and (iv)
d. (i) and (v)

Answers to questions in the chapter

SA1. The correct answer is a.

SA2. The correct answer is a.

SA3. The correct answer is b.

Exercise 4.1

The partitions would be: £0.00–£1,000.00, £1,000.01–£2,000.00, and >= £2,000.01.

Exercise 4.2

The valid partitions would be: £0.00–£20.00, £20.01–£40.00, and >= £40.01.
Non-valid partitions would include negative values and alphabetic characters.

Exercise 4.3

The partitions would be: question scores 0–20; total 0–100; question differences: 0–3 and > 3; total differences 0–10 and > 10.

Boundary values would be: −1, 0, 1 and 19, 20, 21 for the question scores; −1, 0, 1 (again) and 99, 100, 101 for the question paper totals; −1, 0, 1 (again) and 2, 3, 4 for differences between question scores for different markers; and −1, 0, 1 (again) and 9, 10, 11 for total differences between different markers.

In this case, although the −1, 0, 1 values occur several times, they may be applied to different parts of the program (e.g. the question score checks will probably be in a different part of the program from the total score checks) so we may need to repeat these values in the boundary tests.

Exercise 4.4

Billy will be eligible for a cash payment but not for a share allocation.

Exercise 4.5

The correct answer is b.

Answer (a) includes the transition DE; answer (c) includes the transition CE; answer (d) includes the transition FA. None of these is valid from the diagram.

Exercise 4.6

The flow chart is shown in Figure 4.15. The control flow graph is shown in Figure 4.16.

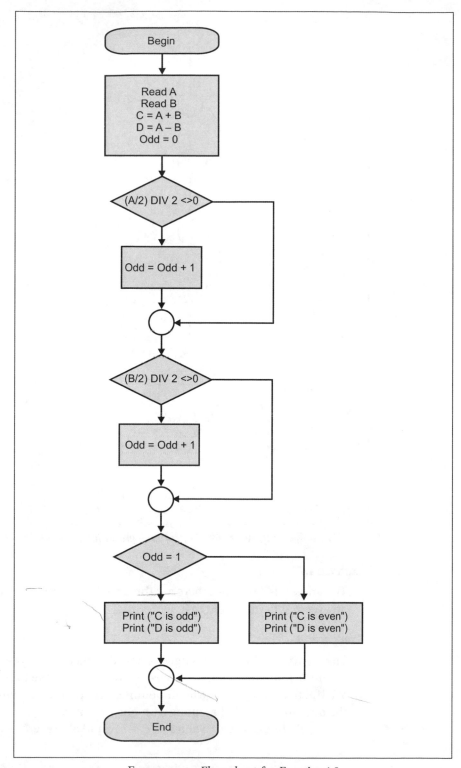

FIGURE 4.15   *Flow chart for Exercise 4.6*

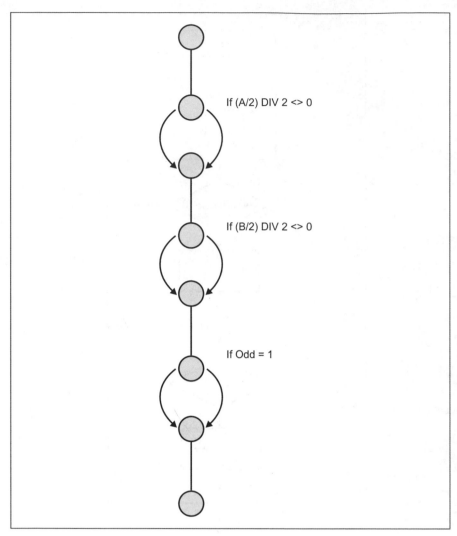

FIGURE 4.16   *Control flow graph for Exercise 4.6*

Exercise 4.7

The answer is 4 because there are three decisions and every outcome has an executable statement in it.

Exercise 4.8

The answer is 1 because a single list terminated by −1 (say 4, 6, 3, −1) will enter the loop the first three times and then exit on the fourth; hence the WHILE decision will be true three times and then false, which exercises the decision in both directions with one test case.

A single test case with values of 1, −1 would also exercise all decisions.

Answers to example questions

E1. The correct answer is c.

Answer (a) relates to specification-based testing, answer (b) relates to experience-based testing and answer (d) could relate either to debugging or to experience-based techniques.

E2. The correct answer is c.

All other options are specification-based (black-box) techniques, and the main distracter is answer (a) because decision table testing could be confused with decision testing.

E3. The correct answer is c.

Answer (a) includes two values from the lower partition, answer (b) contains two values from the second partition, answer (d) contains one value that is invalid (out of range).

E4. The correct answer is b.

The two decisions are in sequence and the conditions are mutually exclusive (if one is true the other must be false). Hence a test case that makes the first decision true will make the second decision false and vice versa. So test case 1 (say 6) would exercise the path True, False, and test case 2 (say 15) would exercise the path False, True. This combination achieves 100 per cent decision coverage because each decision has been exercised through its true and its false outcome.

Note that this piece of pseudo code will not print anything if Time = 12. However, in structure-based testing we are testing the code – not what the code perhaps should do.

E5. The correct answer is a.

Answer (b) relates to integration testing; answer (c) could relate to boundary value analysis or performance testing, but use cases exercise typical process flows rather than extreme examples; answer (d) relates to static analysis.

E6. The correct answer is b.

Answer (i) looks tempting, and the availability of tools might make the use of a technique more or less attractive, but it would not be decisive in the way that regulatory standards and tester knowledge are. Answer (iii) is irrelevant because testing should be independent of development anyway, but it could tempt someone who is unsure about the relationship between development and testing. Answer (v) is a factor in managing the test team, and experience would need to be maintained, but this should not influence the selection of techniques for a live project.

5 Test Management

GEOFF THOMPSON

INTRODUCTION

This chapter provides a generic overview of how testing is organized and how testing is managed within organizations. A generic view of testing will, inevitably, not match the way testing is organized in specific organizations. The issues addressed are nevertheless important for any organization and need to be considered by all.

We will start by looking at how testing and risk fit together, as well as providing detailed coverage of test planning and the control of testing, and we will identify how independence assists the test process. One very important area in managing the test process is the understanding of the different roles and tasks associated with the testing role such as the test leader and the tester.

We cannot, in one chapter, provide all the knowledge required to enable the reader to become a practising test leader or test manager, but we do aim to provide the background information necessary for a reader to understand the various facets of the test management role.

Learning objectives

The learning objectives for this chapter are listed below. You can confirm that you have achieved these by using the self-assessment questions at the start of the chapter, the 'Check of understanding' boxes distributed throughout the text, and the example examination questions provided at the end of the chapter. The chapter summary will remind you of the key ideas.

The sections are allocated a K number to represent the level of understanding required for that section; where an individual has a lower K number than the section as a whole this is indicated for that topic; for an explanation of the K numbers see the Introduction.

Test organization (K2)

- Recognize the importance of independent testing. (K1)
- List the benefits and drawbacks of independent testing within an organization.
- Recognize the different team members to be considered for the creation of a test team. (K1)
- Recall the tasks of typical test leader and tester. (K1)

Test planning and estimation (K2)

- Recognize the different levels and objectives of test planning. (K1)
- Summarize the purpose and content of the test plan, test design specification and test procedure documents according to the 'Standard for Software Test Documentation' (IEEE 829).
- Recall typical factors that influence the effort related to testing. (K1)
- Differentiate between two conceptually different estimation approaches: the metrics-based approach and the expert-based approach.
- Differentiate between the subject of test planning for a project, for individual test levels (e.g. system test) or specific test targets (e.g. usability test), and for test execution.
- List test preparation and execution tasks that need planning. (K1)
- Recognize/justify adequate exit criteria for specific test levels and groups of test cases (e.g. for integration testing, acceptance testing or test cases for usability testing).

Test progress monitoring and control (K2)

- Recall common metrics used for monitoring test preparation and execution. (K1)
- Understand and interpret test metrics for test reporting and test control (e.g. defects found and fixed, and tests passed and failed).
- Summarize the purpose and content of the test summary report document according to the 'Standard for Software Test Documentation' (IEEE 829).

Configuration management (K2)

- Summarize how configuration management supports testing.

Risk and testing (K2)

- Describe a risk as a possible problem that would threaten the achievement of one or more stakeholders' project objectives.
- Remember that risks are determined by likelihood (of happening) and impact (harm resulting if it does happen). (K1)
- Distinguish between the project and product risks.
- Recognize typical product and project risks. (K1)
- Describe, using examples, how risk analysis and risk management may be used for test planning.

Incident management (K3)

- Recognize the content of the 'Standard for Software Test Documentation' (IEEE 829) incident report. (K1)
- Write an incident report covering the observation of a failure during testing.

Self-assessment questions

The following questions have been designed to enable you to check your current level of understanding for the topics in this chapter. The answers are given at the end of the chapter.

Question SA1 (K1)

What is the purpose of exit criteria?

a. To identify how many tests to design.
b. To identify when to start testing.
c. To identify when to stop testing.
d. To identify who will carry out the test execution.

Question SA2 (K2)

Which of the following are **most** likely to be used when developing a test strategy or test approach?

(i) Failure-based approach
(ii) Test specification approach
(iii) Model-based approach
(iv) Finance-based approach

a. (iii) and (ii)
b. (i) and (iv)
c. (ii) and (i)
d. (i) and (iii)

Question SA3 (K1)

What can a risk-based approach to testing provide?

a. The types of test techniques to be employed.
b. The total tests needed to provide 100 per cent coverage.
c. An estimation of the total cost of testing.
d. Only that test execution is effective at reducing risk.

RISK AND TESTING

It is not possible to talk about test management without first looking at risk and how it affects the fundamental test process defined in Chapter 2. If there were no risk of adverse future events in software or hardware development then there would be no need for testing. In other words, if defects did not exist then neither would testing.

Risk can be defined as the chance of an event, hazard, threat, or situation occurring and its undesirable consequences:

> **Risk** – a factor that could result in future negative consequences, usually expressed as impact and likelihood.

In a project a test leader will use risk in two different ways: project risks and product risks. In both instance the calculation of the risk will be:

 Level of risk = probability of the risk occurring × impact if it did happen

Project risks

Whilst managing the testing project a test leader will use project risks to manage the capability to deliver.

Project risks include:

- Supplier issues:
  - ✦ Failure of a third party to deliver on time or at all.
  - ✦ Contractual issues, such as meeting acceptance criteria.
- Organizational factors:
  - ✦ Skill and staff shortages.
  - ✦ Personal and training issues.
  - ✦ Political issues, such as a change of management or restructuring that will affect the project resources.
- Problems that stop testers communicating their needs and test results.
- Failure to follow up on low-level testing and reviews:
  - ✦ Lack of appreciation of the benefits of testing.
- Specialist issues:
  - ✦ Problems in defining the right requirements.
  - ✦ The extent that requirements can be met given existing project constraints.
  - ✦ The quality of the design, development and test team.

For each risk identified a probability (chance of the risk being realized) and impact (what will happen if the risk is realized) should be identified as well as the identification and management of any mitigating actions (actions aimed at reducing the probability of a risk occurring, or reducing the impact of the risk if it did occur).

So, for example if there was a risk identified that the third-party supplier may be made bankrupt during the development, the test manager would review the supplier's accounts and might decide that the probability of this is medium (3 on a scale of 1 to 5, 1 being a high risk and 5 a low one). The impact on the project if this did happen would be very high (1 using the same scale). The level of risk is therefore $3 \times 1 = 3$. Thus, the lower the number, the more the risk. With 3 being in the medium risk area the test leader would now have to consider what mitigating actions to take to try to stop the risk becoming a reality. This might include not using the third party, or ensuring that payment for third-party deliverables is made efficiently.

When analysing, managing and mitigating these risks the test manager is following well-established project management principles provided within project management methods and approaches. The project risks recognized during test planning should be documented in the IEEE 829 test plan (see later in this chapter for details of the test plan contents); for the on-going management and control of existing and new project risks a risk register should be maintained by the test leader.

Product risks

When planning and defining tests a test leader or tester using a risk-based testing approach will be managing product risks.

Potential failure areas (adverse future events or hazards) in software are known as product risks, as they are a risk to the quality of the product. In other words, the potential of a defect occurring in the live environment is a product risk. Examples of product risks are:

- Error-prone software delivered.
- Poor requirements leading to badly defined and built software.
- Potential that a defect in the software/hardware could cause harm to an individual or company.
- Poor software quality characteristics (e.g. functionality, security, reliability, usability, performance) leading to poor user feedback.
- The software does not meet the requirements and delivers functionality that was not requested.

Risks are used to decide where to start testing in the software development life cycle, e.g. the risk of poor requirements could be mitigated by the use of formal reviews as soon as the requirements have been documented at the start of a project. Product risks also provide information enabling decisions regarding how much testing should be carried out on specific components or systems, e.g. the more risk there is, the more detailed and comprehensive the testing may be. In these ways testing is used to reduce the risk of an adverse effect (defect) occurring or being missed.

Mitigating product risks may also involve non-test activities. For example, in the poor requirements situation, a better and more efficient solution may be simply to replace the analyst who is writing the poor requirements in the first place.

As already stated, a risk-based approach to testing provides proactive opportunities to reduce the levels of product risk starting in the initial stages of a project. It involves the identification of product risks and how they are used to guide the test planning, specification and execution. In a risk-based approach the risks identified:

- will determine the test techniques to be employed, and/or the extent of testing to be carried out, e.g. the Motor Industry Software Reliability Association (MISRA) defines which test techniques should be used for each level of risk: the higher the risk, the higher the coverage required from test techniques;

- prioritize testing in an attempt to find the critical defects as early as possible, e.g. by identifying the areas most likely to have defects (the most complex) the testing can be focused on these areas;
- will determine any non-test activities that could be employed to reduce risk, e.g. to provide training to inexperienced designers.

Risk-based testing draws on the collective knowledge and insights of the project stakeholders, testers, designers, technical architects, business reps and anyone with knowledge of the solution to determine the risks and the levels of testing to address those risks.

To ensure that the chance of a product failure is minimized, risk management activities provide a disciplined approach:

- To assess continuously what can go wrong (risks). Regular reviews of the existing and looking for any new product risks should occur periodically throughout the life cycle.
- To determine what risks are important to deal with (probability × impact). As the project progresses, owing to the mitigation activities risks may reduce in importance, or disappear altogether.
- To implement actions to deal with those risks (mitigating actions).

Testing supports the identification of new risks by continually reviewing risks of the project deliverables throughout the life cycle; it may also help to determine what risks are important to reduce by setting priorities; it may lower uncertainty about risks by, for example, testing a component and verifying that it does not contain any defects; and lastly by running specific tests it may verify other strategies that deal with risks, such as contingency plans.

Testing is a risk control activity that provides feedback about the residual risk in the product by measuring the effectiveness of critical defect removal (see below) and by reviewing the effectiveness of contingency plans.

CHECK OF UNDERSTANDING

(1) What are the two types of risks that have to be considered in testing?

(2) Compare and contrast these two risk types.

(3) How early in the life cycle can risk impact the testing approach?

(4) What does MISRA determine when the level of risk is understood?

TEST ORGANIZATION

Test organization and independence

Independent testing is testing carried out by someone other than the creator (developer) of the code being tested. By remaining independent it is possible to improve the effectiveness of testing if implemented correctly.

As humans we are all capable of making mistakes, from the simplest misspelling or wrong use of syntax to fundamental errors at the core of any documents we write. The problem is that as authors we are less able to see our own errors than someone else, who is less directly associated with the document, would be. This is a problem that is made worse, in the world of software development, by the differing 'world view' of testers and developers. A developer, as the creator and owner of documents and code related to development, perceives these deliverables as being correct when they are delivered. The general awareness that we all make mistakes is, at this stage, overridden by the belief that what has been produced is what is required. A tester, by contrast, will take the view that anything delivered for testing is likely to contain errors and will search diligently to identify and locate those errors.

This is where independent testing is important, as it is genuinely hard for authors to identify their own errors, but it is easier for others to see them. There are many options for many levels of independence. In general, the more remote a tester is from the production of the document, the greater is the level of independence. Figure 5.1 indicates the most common roles and the levels of independence they bring.

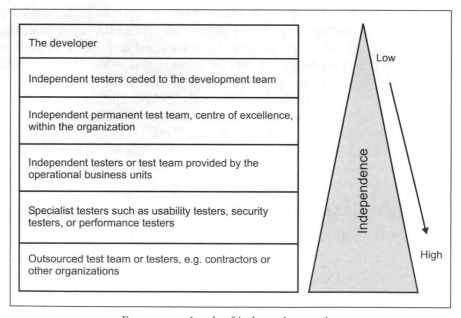

FIGURE 5.1   *Levels of independent testing*

Of course independence comes at a price. The greater the level of independence, the greater the likelihood of errors in testing arising from unfamiliarity. Levels of independence will also depend on the size of the organization. In smaller organizations where everybody contributes to every activity it is harder to differentiate the role of the tester from any other role, and therefore testers may not be very independent at all. The key in these circumstances is for the testers to have independence of mind, not necessarily to be in an independent (separate) team. In organizations where there are clearly defined roles it is a lot easier for a tester to remain independent.

It is also possible to mix and match the levels of independence, e.g. a test team made up of permanent resources, business unit resources and contractors. For large, complex or safety-critical projects, it is usually best to have multiple levels of testing, with some or all of the levels done by independent testers.

The 'agile' approach to development challenges the traditional approach to independence. In this approach everybody takes on multiple roles and so maintaining total independence is not always possible. A tester in this situation has to be able to switch to an independent view, at the relevant points in the project. Testers achieve this independence of view by not assuming anything and by not starting to own the software like a developer would, e.g. the view that that was how it was developed to work

Independence in the implementation of testing has some key benefits and drawbacks, as in Table 5.1.

TABLE 5.1 *Features of independent testing*

Benefits	Drawbacks
The tester sees other and different defects to the author	Isolation from the development team (if treated as totally independent), which will mean the tester is totally dependent on the test basis to understand what it is the tester is testing (documentation that is rarely up to date)
The tester is unbiased	The tester may be seen as the bottleneck, as independent test execution is normally the last stage and affected by any delays earlier in the process testing
The tester can see what has been built rather than what the developer thought had been built	Developers lose a sense of responsibility for quality as it may be assumed that they need not worry about errors because the independent test team will find them
The tester makes no assumptions regarding quality	The fully independent view sets developers and testers on either side of an invisible fence. This can be a hindrance to communication that would in normal circumstances ensure common understanding and effective working. It can also mean that developers are seen to 'throw' the software over the fence

CHECK OF UNDERSTANDING

(1) Why is independent testing more effective at finding errors than simply allowing the developer and author to test their own product?

(2) Name three benefits of independence.

(3) Which organization provides the lowest level of independence and which provides the highest?

Tasks of a test leader and tester

Test tasks are traditionally carried out by people who make testing a career; however, test tasks may also be carried out by non-testers such as a project manager, quality manager, developer, business and domain expert, infrastructure or IT operations. The availability of resources usually determines the resource types that are deployed on each project, e.g. if there are no career testers available an organization may identify non-testing IT or business resources to carry out the role of tester for a specific project or time period.

The syllabus defines two testing roles, the test leader (or test manager/test coordinator) and the tester. Other roles may exist in your organization, but they are not covered here.

The testing roles can be undertaken by anyone with the required skills or who is given the right training. For example, the role of a test leader could be undertaken by a project manager. The decision as to who does what will depend on how a project or organization is structured, as well as the size and number of resources working on a given project.

It is important to understand here the difference between a testing role and a testing job. A role is an activity, or a series of activities given to a person to fulfil, e.g. the role of test leader. A person may therefore have more than one role at any moment depending on their experience and the level of workload on a project. A job is effectively what an individual is employed to do, so one or many roles could make up a job. For example, a test leader could also be a tester.

The tasks undertaken by a test leader align very closely with those undertaken by a project manager and align closely with standard approaches to project management. In this context a test leader is anyone who leads a team of testers (be that one or many testers). They are also known as test programme managers, test managers, test team leaders and test coordinators.

Typical test leader tasks may include:

 • Coordinating the development of the test strategy and plan with project managers and others.

- Writing or reviewing test strategies produced for the project, and test policies produced for the organization.

- Contributing the testing perspective to other project activities, such as development delivery schedules.
- Planning the development of the required tests – which will include ensuring that the development uses the correct understanding of the risks, selecting the required test approaches (test levels, cycles, approach, objectives and incident management planning), estimating the time and effort and converting to the cost of testing and acquiring the right resources.
- Managing the specification, preparation, implementation and execution of tests, including the monitoring and control of all the specification and execution.
- Taking the required action, including adapting the planning, based on test results and progress (sometimes documented in status reports), and any action necessary to compensate for problems or delays.
- Ensuring that adequate configuration management of testware is in place and that the testware is fully traceable, e.g. there is a hierarchical relationship established between the requirements and the detailed specification documents.
- Putting in place suitable metrics for measuring test progress and evaluating the quality of the testing delivered and the product.
- Agreeing what should be automated, to what degree, and how, ensuring it is implemented as planned.
- Where required, selecting tools to support testing and ensuring any tool training requirements are met.
- Agreeing the structure and implementation of the test environment.
- Scheduling all testing activity.
- At the end of the project, writing a test summary report based on the information gathered during testing.

These tasks are not, however, all of the tasks that could be carried out by test leaders, just the most common ones. In fact other resources could take on one or more of these tasks as required, or they may be delegated to other resources by the test leader. The key is to ensure that everyone is aware of who is doing what tasks, that they are completed on time and within budget, and that they are tracked through to completion.

The other role covered by the syllabus is that of the tester, also known as test analyst or test executor.

The tasks typically undertaken by a tester may include:

- Reviewing and contributing to the development of test plans.
- Analysing, reviewing and assessing user requirements, specifications and models for testability.
- Creating test specifications from the test basis.
- Setting up the test environment (often coordinating with system administration and network management). In some organizations the setting up and management of the test environment could be centrally

controlled; in this situation a tester would directly liaise with the environment management to ensure the test environment is delivered on time and to specification.

- Preparing and acquiring/copying/creating test data.
- Implementing tests on all test levels, executing and logging the tests, evaluating the results and documenting the deviations from expected results as defects.
- Using test administration or management and test monitoring tools as required.
- Automating tests (may be supported by a developer or a test automation expert).
- Where required, running the tests and measuring the performance of components and systems (if applicable).
- Reviewing tests developed by other testers.

If specialist testers are not available, then additional resources could be used at different test levels:

- For component and integration testing, any additional roles would typically be filled by someone from a development background.
- For system and user acceptance testing, any additional roles would typically be filled by someone from a business or user background.
- System operators (sometimes known as production support) would be responsible for operational acceptance testing.

As mentioned earlier, the thing to remember when looking at roles and tasks within a test project is that one person may have more than one role and carry out some or all of the tasks applicable to the role. This is different to having a 'job': a 'job' may contain many roles and tasks.

CHECK OF UNDERSTANDING

(1) What other names are given to the test leader role?

(2) Detail five possible tasks of a test leader.

(3) Detail five possible tasks of a tester.

(4) Describe the differences between a test leader role and a test leader task.

TEST APPROACHES (TEST STRATEGIES)

A test approach or test strategy defines how testing will be implemented. A test approach can reflect testing for a whole organization, a programme of work or an individual project. It can be:

- developed early in the life cycle, which is known as preventative – in this approach the test design process is initiated as early as possible in the life cycle to stop defects being built into the final solution;
- left until just before the start of test execution, which is known as reactive – this is where testing is the last development stage and is not started until after design and coding has been completed (sometimes it is identified as the waterfall approach, i.e. all development stages are sequential, the next not starting until the previous one has nearly finished).

There are many approaches or strategies that can be employed including:

- Analytical approaches such as risk-based testing where testing is directed to areas of greatest risk (see later in this section for an overview of risk-based testing).
- Model-based approaches such as stochastic testing using statistical information about failure rates (such as reliability growth models) or usage (such as operational profiles).
- Methodical approaches, such as failure-based (including error guessing and fault attacks), check-list based and quality-characteristic-based.
- Standard-compliant approaches, specified by industry-specific standards such as The Railway Signalling standards (which define the levels of testing required) or the MISRA (which defines how to design, build and test reliable software for the motor industry).
- Process-compliant approaches, which adhere to the processes developed for use with the various agile methodologies or traditional waterfall approaches.
- Dynamic and heuristic approaches, such as exploratory testing (see Chapter 4) where testing is more reactive to events than pre-planned, and where execution and evaluation are concurrent tasks.
- Consultative approaches, such as those where test coverage is driven primarily by the advice and guidance of technology and/or business domain experts outside or within the test team.
- Regression-averse approaches, such as those that include reuse of existing test material, extensive automation of functional regression tests, and standard test suites.

Different approaches may be combined if required. The decision as to how and why they will be combined will depend on the circumstances prevalent in a project at the time. For example, an organization may as a standard use an agile method, but in a particular situation the structure of the test effort could use a risk-based approach to ensure the testing is correctly focused.

Deciding on which approach to take may be dictated by standards, e.g. those used in the motor industry that are set by MISRA, or at the discretion of those developing the approach or strategy. Where discretion is allowed, the context or scenario needs to be taken into account. Therefore the following factors should be considered when defining the strategy or approach:

- Risk of failure of the project, hazards to the product and risks of product failure to humans, the environment and the company, e.g. the cost of failure would be too high (safety critical environments).

- Skills and experience of the people in the proposed techniques, tools and methods. There is no point in implementing a sophisticated component-level, technique-driven approach or strategy when the only resources available are business users with no technical grounding.

- The objective of the testing endeavour and the mission of the testing team, e.g. if the objective is to find only the most serious defects.

- Regulatory aspects, such as external and internal regulations for the development process, e.g. The Railway Signalling standards that enforce a given level of test quality.

- The nature of the product and the business, e.g. a different approach is required for testing mobile phone coverage than for testing an online banking operation.

CHECK OF UNDERSTANDING

(1) Name and explain five approaches to the development of the test approach or test strategy.

(2) Name one of the standards referred to that dictate the test approach.

(3) Can discretion be used when defining a test approach and if so what can influence the decision as to which way to approach testing?

TEST PLANNING AND ESTIMATION

Test planning

Test planning is the most important activity undertaken by a test leader in any test project. It ensures that there is initially a list of tasks and milestones in a baseline plan to track progress against, as well as defining the shape and size of the test effort. Test planning is used in development and implementation projects (sometimes called 'green field') as well as maintenance (change and fix) activities.

The main document produced in test planning is often called a master test plan or a project test plan. This document defines the high level of the test activities being planned. It is normally produced during the early phases of the project (e.g. initiation) and will provide sufficient information to enable a test project to be established (bearing in mind that at this point in a project little more than requirements may be available from which to plan).

The details of the test-level activities are documented within test-level plans, e.g. the system test plan. These documents will contain the detailed activities and estimates for the relevant test level.

Figure 5.2 shows where test-level test plans fit into the V-model. It shows how a test plan exists for each test level and that they will usually refer to the master test plan.

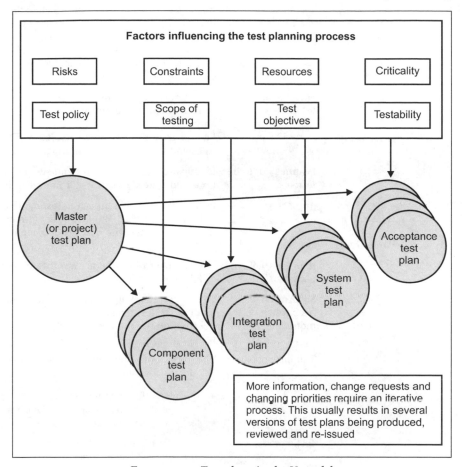

FIGURE 5.2   *Test plans in the V-model*

The contents sections of a test plan for either the master test plan or test-level plans are normally identical or very similar. IEEE 829, the Standard for Software Test Documentation, contains details of what the content of the plans should be.

The IEEE 829 standard identifies that there should be a minimum of 16 sections present in a test plan, as in Table 5.2.

Test planning is a continual activity that spans the life of the test project; it takes place in all life-cycle stages. As risks and changes occur, the plan and planning should be amended to recognize these and reflect the current position. As the plans will have been baselined (locked down) after initial

TABLE 5.2   *Test plan sections*

Section no.	Heading	Details
1	Test plan identifier	A unique identifying reference such as 'Doc ref XYZ v2'
2	Introduction	A brief introduction to the document and the project for which it has been produced
3	Test items	A test item is a software item which is the object of testing A software item is one or more items of source code, object code, job control code, or control data This section should contain any documentation references, e.g. design documents
4	Features to be tested	A feature is a distinguishing characteristic of a software item (e.g. performance, portability, or functionality) Identify all software features and combinations of features and the associated test design specification
5	Features not to be tested	Identify all software features and significant combinations and state the reasons for not including them
6	Approach	Details the overall approach to testing; this could include a detailed process definition, or could refer to other documentation where the detail is documented, i.e. a test strategy
7	Item pass/fail criteria	Used to determine whether a software item has passed or failed its test
8	Suspension and resumption requirements	Suspension requirements define criteria for stopping part or all of the testing activity Resumption requirements specify the requirements to resume testing
9	Test deliverables	The documents which testing will deliver, e.g. from IEEE 829 documents such as: • test plans (for each test level) • test specifications (design, case and procedure) • test summary reports
10	Testing tasks	All tasks for planning and executing the testing, including the intertask dependencies
11	Environmental needs	Definition of all environmental requirements such as hardware, software, PCs, desks, stationery, etc.
12	Responsibilities	Identifies the roles and tasks to be used in the test project and who will own them
13	Staffing and training needs	Identifies any actual staffing requirements and any specific skills and training requirements, e.g. automation
14	Schedule	Document delivery dates and key milestones
15	Risks and contingencies	High-level project risks and assumptions and a contingency plan for each risk
16	Approvals	Identifies all approvers of the document, their titles and the date of signature

sign-off, these changes would normally be managed by the project change process. Baselining a document effectively secures it from further change unless authorised via a change control process.

A useful revision aid to help remember the 16 sections of the IEEE 829 test plan is the acronym 'SPACEDIRT', each letter mapping to one or several sections of the test plan:

S   scope (including test items, features to be tested and features not to be tested)

P   people (including responsibilities, staff and training and approvals)

A   approach

C   criteria (including item pass/fail criteria and suspension and resumption requirements)

E   environment needs

D   deliverables (test)

I   identifier and introduction (test plan)

R   risks and contingencies

T   testing tasks and schedule

Test-planning activities

During test planning various activities have to be undertaken by those working on the plan. They include:

- Putting together the overall approach of testing (sometimes called the test strategy), ensuring that the test levels and entry and exit criteria are defined.
- Liaising with the project manager and making sure that the testing activities have been included within the software life-cycle activities such as:
    + design – the development of the software design;
    + development – the building of the code;
    + implementation – the activities surrounding implementation into a live environment.
- Working with the project to decide what needs to be tested, what roles are involved and who will perform the test activities, planning when and how the test activities should be done, deciding how the test results will be evaluated, and defining when to stop testing (exit criteria).
- Finding and assigning resources for the different tasks that have been defined.

- Deciding what the documentation for the test project will be, e.g. which plans, how the test cases will be documented, etc.
- Defining the management information, including the metrics required and putting in place the processes to monitor and control test preparation and execution, defect resolution and risk issues.
- Ensuring that the test documentation generates repeatable test assets, e.g. test cases.

Exit criteria

Exit criteria are used to determine when a given test activity has been completed or when it should stop. Exit criteria can be defined for all of the test activities, such as planning, specification and execution as a whole, or to a specific test level for test specification as well as execution.

Exit criteria should be included in the relevant test plans.

Some typical exit criteria might be:

- All tests planned have been run.
- A certain level of requirements coverage has been achieved.
- No high-priority or severe defects are left outstanding.
- All high-risk areas have been fully tested, with only minor residual risks left outstanding.
- Cost – when the budget has been spent.
- The schedule has been achieved, e.g. the release date has been reached and the product has to go live. This was the case with the millennium testing (it had to be completed before midnight on 31 December 1999), and is often the case with government legislation.

Exit criteria should have been agreed as early as possible in the life cycle; however, they can be and often are subject to controlled change as the detail of the project becomes better understood and therefore the ability to meet the criteria is better understood by those responsible for delivery.

CHECK OF UNDERSTANDING

(1) What is the name of the international standard for test documentation?

(2) Identify the 16 sections of the test plan.

(3) What activities are contained within test planning?

(4) Detail four typical exit criteria.

Test estimation

The syllabus details two test estimation approaches, metrics-based and expert-based. The two approaches are quite different, the former being based upon data whilst the latter is a somewhat subjective approach.

The metrics-based approach — data.

This approach relies upon data collected from previous or similar projects. This kind of data might include:

- The number of test conditions.
- The number of test cases written.
- The number of test cases executed.
- The time taken to develop test cases.
- The time taken to run test cases.
- The number of defects found.
- The number of environment outages and how long on average each one lasted.

With this approach and data it is possible to estimate quite accurately what the cost and time required for a similar project would be.

It is important that the actual costs and time for testing are accurately recorded. These can then be used to revalidate and possibly update the metrics for use on the next similar project.

The expert-based approach 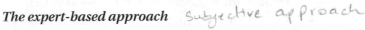 subjective approach

This alternative approach to metrics is to use the experience of owners of the relevant tasks or experts to derive an estimate (this is also known as the Wide Band Delphi approach). In this context 'experts' could be:

- Business experts.
- Test process consultants.
- Developers.
- Technical architects.
- Analysts and designers.
- Anyone with knowledge of the application to be tested or the tasks involved in the process.

There are many ways that this approach could be used. Here are two examples:

- Distribute a requirements specification to the task owners and get them to estimate for their task in isolation. Amalgamate the individual estimates when received; build in any required contingency, to arrive at the estimate.
- Distribute to known experts who develop their individual view of the overall estimate and then meet together to agree on and/or debate the estimate that will go forward.

Expert estimating can use either of the above approaches individually or mixing and matching them as required.

Many things affect the level of effort required to fulfil the test requirements of a project. These can be split into three main categories, as shown below.

- Product characteristics:

- ✦ size of the test basis;
- ✦ complexity of the final product;
- ✦ the amount of non-functional requirements;
- ✦ the security requirements (perhaps meeting BS 7799, the security standard);
- ✦ how much documentation is required (e.g. some legislation-driven changes demand a certain level of documentation which may be more than an organization would normally produce);
- ✦ the availability and quality of the test basis (e.g. requirements and specifications).
- Development process characteristics:
  - ✦ timescales;
  - ✦ amount of budget available;
  - ✦ skills of those involved in the testing and development activity (the lower the skill level in development, the more defects could be introduced, and the lower the skill level in testing, the more detailed the test documentation needs to be);
  - ✦ which tools are being used across the life cycle (i.e. the amount of automated testing will affect the effort required).
- Expected outcome of testing such as:
  - ✦ the amount of errors;
  - ✦ test cases to be written.

Taking all of this into account, once the estimate is developed and agreed the test leader can set about identifying the required resources and building the detailed plan.

CHECK OF UNDERSTANDING

(1) Compare and contrast the two approaches to developing estimates.

(2) Provide three examples of what a metrics approach to estimates would use as a base.

(3) Name three areas that affect the level of effort to complete the test activity.

TEST PROGRESS MONITORING AND CONTROL

Test progress monitoring

Having developed the test plan, the activities and timescales determined within it need to be constantly reviewed against what is actually happening. This is test progress monitoring. The purpose of test progress monitoring is to provide feedback and visibility of the progress of test activities.

The data required to monitor progress can be collected manually, e.g. counting test cases developed at the end of each day, or, with the advent of sophisticated test management tools, it also possible to collect the data as an automatic output from a tool either already formatted into a report, or as a data file that can be manipulated to present a picture of progress.

The progress data is also used to measure exit criteria such as test coverage, e.g. 50 per cent requirements coverage achieved.

Common test metrics include:

- Percentage of work done in test case preparation (or percentage of planned test cases prepared).
- Percentage of work done in test environment preparation.
- Test case execution (e.g. number of test cases run/not run, and test cases passed/failed).
- Defect information (e.g. defect density, defects found and fixed, failure rate and retest results).
- Test coverage of requirements, risks or code.
- Subjective confidence of testers in the product.
- Dates of test milestones.
- Testing costs, including the cost compared with the benefit of finding the next defect or to run the next test.

Ultimately test metrics are used to track progress towards the completion of testing, which is determined by the exit criteria. So test metrics should relate directly to the exit criteria.

There is a trend towards 'dashboards', which reflect all of the relevant metrics on a single screen or page, ensuring maximum impact. For a dashboard, and generally when delivering metrics, it is best to use a relatively small but impact-worthy subset of the various metric options available. This is because the readers do not want to wade through lots of data for the key item of information they are after, which invariably is 'Are we on target to complete on time?'

These metrics are often displayed in graphical form, examples of which are shown in Figure 5.3. This reflects progress on the running of test cases and reports on defects found. There is also a box at the top left for some written commentary on progress to be documented (this could simply be the issues and/or successes of the previous reporting period).

The graph in Figure 5.4 is the one shown at the bottom left of the dashboard in Figure 5.3. It reports the number of incidents raised, and also shows the planned and actual numbers of incidents.

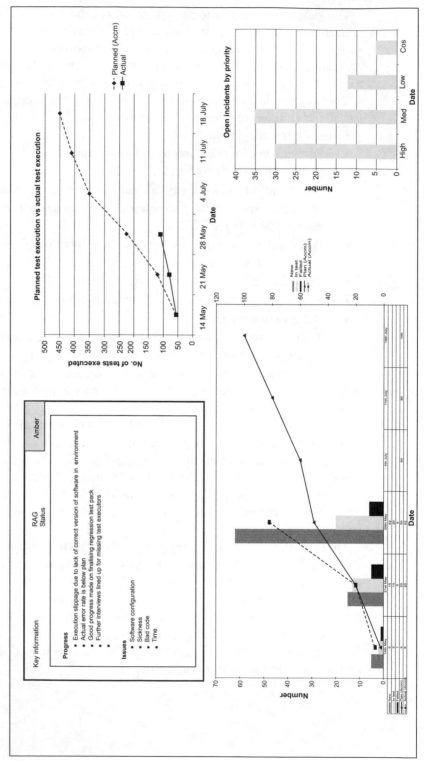

FIGURE 5.3　iTesting Executive Dashboard

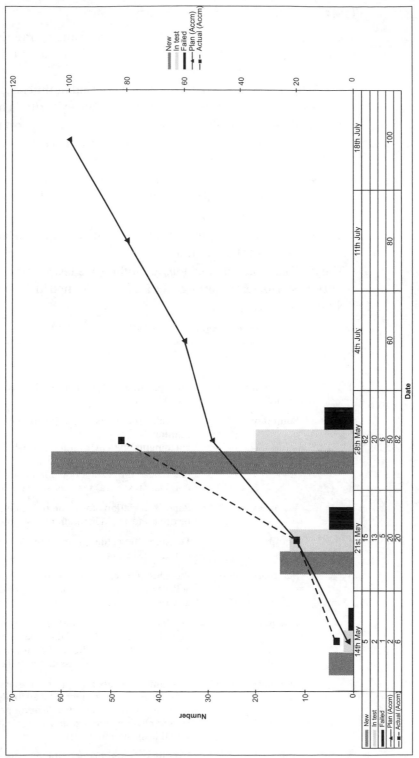

FIGURE 5.4   *Incidents planned/raised*

Test reporting

Test reporting is the process whereby test metrics are reported in summarized format to update the reader regarding the testing tasks undertaken. The information reported can include:

- What has happened during a given period of time, e.g. a week, a test level or the whole test endeavour, or when exit criteria have been met.
- Analysed information and metrics required to support recommendations and decisions about future actions, such as:
  - ✦ an assessment of defects remaining;
  - ✦ the economic benefit of continued testing, e.g. additional tests are exponentially more expensive than the benefit of running;
  - ✦ outstanding risks;
  - ✦ the level of confidence in tested software, e.g. defects planned vs actual defects found

The IEEE 829 standard includes an outline of a test summary report which could be used for test reporting. The structure defined in the outline is shown in Table 5.3.

TABLE 5.3 *Test summary report outline*

Section no.	Heading	Details
1	Test summary report identifier	The specific identifier allocated to this document, e.g. TSR XYX v1
2	Summary	Identifies the items tested (including any version numbers) Documents the environments in which the test activity being reported on took place References the testing documentation for each test item, e.g. test plan, test cases, test defect reports
3	Variances	Reports deviations from the test approach or strategy, test plan, test specification or test procedures
4	Comprehensive assessment	Measures the actual progress made against the exit criteria and explains why any differences have arisen
5	Summary results	Provides an overview of the results from the test activities; it should include details of defects raised and fixed, as well as those that remain unresolved
6	Evaluation	Provides an evaluation of the quality of each test item, including a view of the risks of failure in production of these test items. Based upon the test result metrics and test item pass/fail criteria
7	Summary of activities	A summary of the major test activities and events such as test environment unavailability, success or weaknesses of the test specification process, etc. Should also include resource usage data, e.g. planned spend against actual spend
8	Approvals	Identifies all approvers of the document

The information gathered can also be used to help with any process improvement opportunities. This information could be used to assess whether:

- the goals for testing were correctly set (were they achievable; if not why not?);
- the test approach or strategy was adequate (e.g. did it ensure there was enough coverage?);
- the testing was effective in ensuring that the objectives of testing were met.

Test control

We have referred above to the collection and reporting of progress data. Test control uses this information to decide on a course of action to ensure control of the test activities is maintained and exit criteria are met. This is particularly required when the planned test activities are behind schedule. The actions taken could impact any of the test activities and may also affect other software life-cycle activities.

Examples of test-control activities are as follows:

- Reprioritize tests when an identified project risk occurs (e.g. software delivered late).
- Change the test schedule due to availability of a test environment.
- Set an entry criterion requiring fixes to be retested by a developer before accepting them into a build (this is particularly useful when defect fixes continually fail again when retested).
- Review of product risks and perhaps changing the risk ratings to meet the target.
- Adjusting the scope of the testing (perhaps the amount of tests to be run) to manage the testing of late change requests.

The following test-control activities are likely to be outside the test leader's responsibility. However, this should not stop the test leader making a recommendation to the project manager.

- Descoping of functionality, i.e. removing some less important planned deliverables from the initial delivered solution to reduce the time and effort required to achieve that solution.
- Delaying release into the production environment until exit criteria have been met.
- Continuing testing after delivery into the production environment so that defects are found before they occur in production.

CHECK OF UNDERSTANDING

(1) Name four common test metrics.

(2) Name the eight headings in the IEEE 829 summary report.

(3) Identify three ways a test leader can control testing if there are more tests than there is time to complete.

INCIDENT MANAGEMENT

An incident is any unplanned event occurring that requires further investigation. In testing this translates into anything where the actual result is different to the expected result.

Incidents can be raised at any time throughout the software development life cycle, from reviews of the test basis (requirements, specifications, etc.) to test specification and test execution.

Incident management, according to IEEE 1044 (Standard Classification for Software Anomalies), is 'The process of recognizing, investigating, taking action and disposing of incidents.' It involves recording incidents, classifying them and identifying the impact. The process of incident management ensures that incidents are tracked from recognition to correction, and finally through retest and closure. It is important that organizations document their incident management process and ensure they have appointed someone (often called an incident manager/coordinator) to manage/police the process.

Incidents are raised on incident reports, either electronically via an incident management system (from Microsoft Excel to sophisticated incident management tools) or on paper. Incident reports have the following objectives:

- To provide developers and other parties with feedback on the problem to enable identification, isolation and correction as necessary. It must be remembered that most developers and other parties who will correct the defect or clear up any confusion will not be present at the point of identification, so without full and concise information they will be unable to understand the problem, and possibly therefore unable to understand how to go about fixing it. The more information provided, the better.

- To provide test leaders with a means of tracking the quality of the system under test and the progress of the testing. One of the key metrics used to measure progress is a view of how many incidents are raised, their priority and finally that they have been corrected and signed off.

- To provide ideas for test process improvement. For each incident the point of injection should be documented, e.g. a defect in requirements or code, and subsequent process improvement can focus on that particular area to stop the same defect occurring again.

The details that are normally included on an incident report are:

- Date of issue, issuing organization, author, approvals and status.
- Scope, severity and priority of the incident.
- References, including the identity of the test case specification that revealed the problem.
- Expected and actual results.
- Date the incident was discovered.
- Identification or configuration item of the software or system.
- Software or system life-cycle process in which the incident was observed.
- Description of the anomaly to enable resolution.
- Degree of impact on stakeholder(s) interests.
- Severity of the impact on the system.
- Urgency/priority to fix.
- Status of the incident (e.g. open, deferred, duplicate, waiting to be fixed, fixed awaiting confirmation test or closed).
- Conclusions and recommendations.
- Global issues, such as other areas that may be affected by a change resulting from the incident.
- Change history, such as the sequence of actions taken by project team members with respect to the incident to isolate, repair and confirm it as fixed.

The syllabus also recognizes that IEEE 829 contains the outline of a test incident report. The outline suggests that the report should contain the sections shown in Table 5.4.

TABLE 5.4   *Test incident report outline*

Section no.	Heading	Details
1	Test incident report identifier	The unique identifier assigned to this test incident report
2	Summary	A summary of the incident, detailing where expected and actual results differ, identifying at a high level the items that are affected, and the steps leading up to the recognition of the incident, e.g. if in test execution, which test was executed and the actual keystrokes and data loaded

Section no.	Heading	Details
3	Incident description	A detailed description of the incident, which should include: • Inputs • Expected results • Actual results • Anomalies • Date and time • Procedure step • Environment • Attempts to repeat • Testers' comments • Observers' comments Should also include any information regarding possible causes and solutions
4	Impact	If known, document what impact the incident has on progress

CHECK OF UNDERSTANDING

(1) Identify three details that are usually included in an incident report.
(2) What is the name of the standard that includes an outline of a test incident report?
(3) What is a test incident?

CONFIGURATION MANAGEMENT

Configuration management is the process of managing products, facilities and processes by managing the information about them, including changes, and ensuring they are what they are supposed to be in every case.

For testing, configuration management will involve controlling both the versions of code to be tested and the documents used during the development process, e.g. requirements, design and plans.

In both instances configuration management should ensure traceability throughout the test process, e.g. a requirement should be traceable through to the test cases that are run to test its levels of quality, and vice versa.

Effective configuration management is important for the test process as the contents of each release of software into a test environment must be understood and at the correct version, otherwise testers could end up wasting time because either they are testing an invalid release of the software or the release does not integrate successfully, leading to the failure of many tests.

In most instances the project will have already established its configuration management processes which will define the documents and code to be held under configuration management. If this is not the case then during test planning the process and tools required to establish the right configuration management processes will need to be selected/implemented by the test leader.

The same principle applies to testware. Each item of testware (such as a test procedure) should have its own version number and be linked to the version for the software it was used to test. For example, test procedure TP123a might be used for Release A and TP123b might be used for Release B – even though both have the same purpose and even expected results. However, another test procedure, TP201, may be applicable to all releases.

A good configuration management system will ensure that the testers can identify exactly what code they are testing, as well as have control over the test documentation such as test plans, test specification, defect logs, etc.

CHECK OF UNDERSTANDING

(1) Define configuration management.

(2) What can be stored under configuration management?

(3) Why is it important to have effective configuration management?

SUMMARY

In this chapter we have looked at the component parts of test management. We initially explored risk and testing. When developing the test plan, the test leader and tester will look at the product risks (risks that relate directly to the failure of the product in the live environment) to decide what is important to test, as well as ensuring that any project risks (risks relating to the delivery of the project) are mitigated.

The importance of independence in the test organization and how independence helps to ensure that the right focus is given to the test activity was reviewed. Independence is gained by separating the creative development activity from the test activity and we looked at the different levels of independence that are achievable:

- The developers – low independence.
- Independent testers ceded to the development team.
- Independent permanent test team, centre of excellence with the organization.

- Independent testers or test team provided by the operational business unit.
- Specialist testers such as security testers or performance testers.
- Outsourced test team or the use of independent contractors – high independence.

We have reviewed two roles that exist within a test project, test leader (also known as a test manager or test coordinator) and tester. Both roles are important to the delivery of testing, but could be vested in one or many people, e.g. one person could have the role of test manager and tester. A test leader has responsibility for all of the planning activity, whilst the tester has responsibility for activities that surround the preparation of test cases.

IEEE 829, the test documentation standard, provides outlines of three test planning documents:

- The test plan
- The test summary report
- The test incident report

Test management depends not only on the preparation of the required documents but also on the development of the right estimate, the monitoring of progress through the plan and the control activities implemented to ensure the plan is achieved.

Test estimating can be achieved in one of two ways, using historical metrics or the expert-based approach (involving experts in the subject who agree the estimate between them).

After a plan of activity has been developed and time begins to pass the test leader needs to monitor the progress of the activities. If any activity is delayed or there has been a change of any kind in the project itself, the test leader may need to revise the plan or take other actions to ensure the project is delivered on time.

We explored how the incidents found during testing are recorded, and we reviewed the level of detail that needs to be recorded to ensure that any defect is fully understood and that any fix then made is the right one.

Finally we looked at configuration management. When running test cases against the code it is important that the tester is aware of the version of code being tested and the version of the test being run. Controlling the versioning of the software and test assets is called configuration management. Lack of configuration management may lead to issues like loss of already-delivered functionality, reappearance of previously corrected errors and no understanding of which version of test was run against which version of code.

Example Examination Questions with Answers

E1. *K1 question*

When assembling a test team to work on an enhancement to an existing system, which of the following has the highest level of test independence?

a.   A business analyst who wrote the original requirements for the system.
b.   A permanent programmer who reviewed some of the new code, but has not written any of it.
c.   A permanent tester who found most defects in the original system.
d.   A contract tester who has never worked for the organization before.

E2. *K2 question*

What test roles (or parts in the testing process) is a developer **most likely** to perform?

(i)   Executing component integration tests.
(ii)   Static analysis.
(iii) Setting up the test environment.
(iv) Deciding how much testing should be automated.

a.   (i) and (ii)
b.   (i) and (iv)
c.   (ii) and (iii)
d.   (iii) and (iv)

E3. *K2 question*

Which of the following are valid justifications for developers testing their own code during unit testing?

(i)   Their lack of independence is mitigated by independent testing during system and acceptance testing.
(ii)   A person with a good understanding of the code can find more defects more quickly using white-box techniques.
(iii) Developers have a better understanding of the requirements than testers.
(iv) Testers write unnecessary incident reports because they find minor differences between the way in which the system behaves and the way in which it is specified to work.

a.   (i) and (ii)
b.   (i) and (iv)
c.   (ii) and (iii)
d.   (iii) and (iv)

E4. *K1 question*

Which of the following terms is used to describe the management of software components comprising an integrated system?

a.   Configuration management
b.   Incident management

    c.   Test monitoring

    d.   Risk management

E5.

A new system is about to be developed. Which of the following functions has the **highest** level of risk?

    a.   likelihood of failure = 20%; impact value = £100,000

    b.   likelihood of failure = 10%; impact value = £150,000

    c.   likelihood of failure = 1%; impact value = £500,000

    d.   likelihood of failure = 2%; impact value = £200,000

E6.

Which of the following statements about risks is most accurate?

    a.   Project risks rarely affect product risk.

    b.   Product risks rarely affect project risk.

    c.   A risk-based approach is more likely to be used to mitigate product rather than project risks.

    d.   A risk-based approach is more likely to be used to mitigate project rather than product risks.

Answers to questions in the chapter

SA1. The correct answer is c.

SA2. The correct answer is d.

SA3. The correct answer is a.

Answers to example questions

E1. The correct answer is d.

In this scenario, the contract tester who has never worked for the organiz-ation before has the highest level of test independence. The three others are less independent as they are likely to make assumptions based on their previous knowledge of the requirements, code and general functionality of the original system.

Note that independence does not necessarily equate to most useful. In practice most test or project managers would recruit a permanent tester who has worked on the original system in preference to a contract tester with no knowledge of the system. However, when assembling a team it would be useful to have staff with varying levels of test independence and system knowledge.

E2. The correct answer is a.

(i) Executing component integration tests is usually done by developers. Developers are usually responsible for unit and component integ-ration testing. Independent testing usually follows at system and acceptance test levels.

(ii) Static analysis is usually done by developers because: it requires an understanding of the code and therefore the person doing this needs skills in the programming language; and it can be done as soon as the code is written. Therefore it is quick and effective for the developer to do it. The risk of a lack of test independence can be mitigated by performing independent system and acceptance testing.

(iii) Setting up the test environment is an activity typically performed by a tester. It may require support from developers and staff from other departments and on some occasions environments could be set up by developers. However, it is a task that could be done by a tester rather than a developer.

(iv) Deciding how much testing should be automated is typically a decision made by the test leader, who will consult other staff in the decision-making process. Developers may be involved and their skills may be required to automate some tests. However, the decision on how much to automate should not be made by developers.

E3. The correct answer is a.

It is unlikely that developers will have a better understanding of the requirements than testers, partly because testers work closely with the user community (and may be drawn from it) and partly because developers seldom work with the complete set of requirements in a medium to large development.

Testers may raise incidents related to the difference between user expectations and the specification, but these are not unnecessary. Such issues are more likely to arise at the later stages of testing.

Early testing (unit testing) is usually done most effectively by developers with a good understanding of the code and the development environment; they can be more efficient and more effective at this level. Later independent stages of testing offset any disadvantage from the lack of independence at unit testing level.

E4. The correct answer is a.

Incident management is the collection and processing of incidents raised when errors and defects are discovered. Test monitoring identifies the status of the testing activity on a continuous basis. Risk management identifies, analyses and mitigates risks to the project and the product. Configuration management is concerned with the management of changes to software components and their associated documentation and testware.

E5. The correct answer is a.

In (b) the product of probability × impact has the value £15,000; in (c) the value is £5,000 and in (d) it is £4,000. The value of £20,000 in (a) is therefore the highest.

E6. The correct answer is c.

In general, project risk and product risk can be hard to differentiate. Anything that impacts on the quality of the delivered system is likely to lead to delays or increased costs as the problem is tackled. Anything causing delays to the project is likely to threaten the delivered system's quality. The risk-based approach is an approach to managing product risk through testing, so it impacts most directly on product risk.

6 Tool Support for Testing

PETER WILLIAMS

INTRODUCTION

As seen in earlier chapters there are many tasks and activities that need to be performed during the testing process. In addition, other tasks need to be performed to support the testing process.

In order to assist in making the testing process easier to perform and manage, many different types of test tools have been developed and used for a wide variety of testing tasks. Some of them have been developed in house by an organization's own software development or testing department. Others have been developed by software houses (also known as test-tool vendors) to sell to organizations that perform testing. Even within the same type of tool, some will be home-grown and others will be developed by test-tool vendors.

This chapter discusses the potential benefits and pitfalls associated with test tools in general. It then describes the most commonly used types of test tools and concludes with a process for introducing a tool into a test organization.

Learning objectives

The learning objectives for this chapter are listed below. You can confirm that you have achieved these by using the self-assessment questions at the start of the chapter, the 'Check of understanding' boxes distributed throughout the text, and the example examination questions provided at the end of the chapter. The chapter summary will remind you of the key ideas.

The sections are allocated a K number to represent the level of understanding required for that section; where an individual section has a lower K number than the section as a whole this is indicated for that topic; for an explanation of the K numbers see the Introduction.

Types of test tool (K2)
- Classify different types of test tools according to the test process activities. (K2)
- Recognize tools that may help developers in their testing. (K1)

Effective use of tools: potential benefits and risks (K2)
- Summarize the potential benefits and risks of test automation and tool support for testing. (K2)
- Recognize that test execution tools can have different scripting techniques, including data driven and keyword driven. (K1)

Introducing a tool into an organization (K1)

- State the main principles of introducing a tool into an organization. (K1)
- State the goals of a proof-of-concept/piloting phase for tool evaluation. (K1)
- Recognize that factors other than simply acquiring a tool are required for good tool support.(K1)

Self-assessment questions

The following questions have been designed to enable you to check your current level of understanding for the topics in this chapter. The answers are at the end of the chapter.

Question SA1 (K2)

Which of the following pairs of test tools are **likely** to be **most useful** during the test analysis and design stage of the fundamental test process?

(i)   Test execution tool
(ii) Test data preparation tool
(iii) Test management tool
(iv) Requirements management tool

a.   (i) and (ii)
b.   (i) and (iv)
c.   (ii) and (iii)
d.   (iii) and (iv)

Question SA2 (K2)

Which of the following is **most likely** to cause failure in the implementation of a test tool?

a.   Underestimating the demand for a tool.
b.   The purchase price of the tool.
c.   No agreed requirements for the tool.
d.   The cost of resources to implement and maintain the tool.

Question SA3 (K2)

What benefits do static analysis tools have over test execution tools?

a.   Static analysis tools find defects earlier in the life cycle.
b.   Static analysis tools can be used before code is written.
c.   Static analysis tools test that the delivered code meets business requirements.
d.   Static analysis tools are particularly effective for regression testing.

WHAT IS A TEST TOOL?

Definition of a test tool

The ISTQB Glossary of Testing Terms v1.1 defines a test tool as:

> A software product that supports one or more test activities, such as planning and control, specification, building initial files and data, test execution and test analysis.

Therefore a test tool can be thought of as a piece of software that is used to make the testing process more effective or efficient. In other words, anything that makes testing easier, quicker, more accurate, etc.

This book will focus on those test tools that are listed in the ISTQB Foundation Level Syllabus, version 2005, 1/7/2005. These are, in general, the test tools that are most commonly used in the testing process and designed primarily for the testing process.

Benefits and risks of using any type of tool

Let us consider the building of a new hotel and examine the similarities with the introduction and use of test tools. Test tools need to be thought of as long-term investments that need maintenance to provide long-term benefits. Similarly, building a hotel requires a lot of upfront planning, effort and investment. Even when the hotel is ready for use, there is still a continual long-term requirement for the provision of services such as catering, cleaning, building maintenance, provision of staff to provide ad hoc services to customers, etc. The long-term benefit is that this upfront investment and on-going maintenance and support can provide substantial income in return.

In addition, there are risks that over a period of time, the location of the hotel will become less attractive, resulting in lower demand, lower usage and a maintenance cost that is greater than the income received. Therefore the initial investment is wasted because the on-going need/requirement did not exist.

The graph in Figure 6.1 demonstrates a typical payback model for implementing a test execution tool. The same principle applies to the majority of test tools. Note that there is an on-going maintenance cost of using the tool, but that this on-going maintenance cost needs to be less than the cost of performing testing activities without the tool if the investment is to be worthwhile.

The same advantages and disadvantages apply to the use of most types of test tool. However, there are exceptions to this generalization (and to the same generalization made in the ISTQB syllabus). Some tools, such as comparators, can be used virtually straight out of the box. A comparator can check whether one large test file is the same as another. If it is different it can identify and report upon the differences. This would be very difficult and

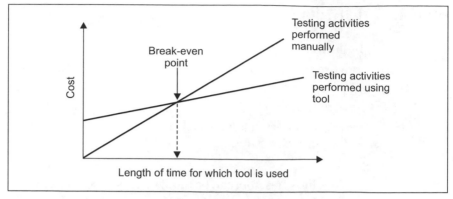

FIGURE 6.1 *Test tool payback model*

time consuming to do manually. In addition, incident management tools are fairly intuitive and easy for both experienced and novice testers to use. They are also likely to provide a 'quick win'.

Other tools can be built by developers in-house as the need arises. For instance, test harnesses, test oracles or test data preparation tools may be relatively easy to produce for developers with a good understanding of the tool requirements and the systems and databases in the test environment.

Benefits

The main benefit of using test tools is similar to the main benefit of automating any process. That is, the amount of time and effort spent performing routine, mundane, repetitive tasks is greatly reduced. For example, consider the time and cost of making consumer goods by hand or in a factory.

This time saved can be used to reduce the costs of testing or it can be used to allow testers to spend more time on the more intellectual tasks of test planning, analysis and design. In turn, this can enable more focused and appropriate testing to be done – rather than having many testers working long hours, running hundreds of tests.

Related to this is the fact that the automation of any process usually results in more predictable and consistent results. Similarly, the use of test tools provides more predictable and consistent results as human failings such as manual-keying errors, misunderstandings, incorrect assumptions, forgetfulness, etc., are eliminated. It also means that any reports or findings tend to be objective rather than subjective. For instance, humans often assume that something that seems reasonable is correct, when in fact it may not be what the system is supposed to do.

The widespread use of databases to hold the data input, processed or captured by the test tool, means that it is generally much easier and quicker to obtain and present accurate test management information, such as test progress, incidents found/fixed, etc. (see Chapter 5).

Risks

Most of the risks associated with the use of test tools are concerned with over-optimistic expectations of what the tool can do and a lack of appreciation of the effort required to implement and obtain the benefits that the tool can bring.

For example, consider the production environments of most organizations considering using test tools. They are unlikely to have been designed and built with test tools in mind. Therefore, assuming that you want a test environment to be a copy of production (or at least as close to it as possible), you will also have a test environment that is not designed and built with test tools in mind.

Consider the test environments used by vendors to demonstrate their test tools. If you were the vendor would you design the environment to enable you to demonstrate the tool at its best or to demonstrate the shortcomings it may encounter in a typical test environment?

Therefore, unless detailed analysis and evaluation is done, it is likely that test tools will end up as something that seemed a good idea at the time but have been largely a waste of time and money. A process for avoiding such problems when introducing a tool into an organization is described later in this chapter.

EXAMPLE – HOTEL CHAIN SCENARIO

An example of a hotel chain with several UK-based hotels will be used throughout this chapter. The systems that comprise the organization's system architecture are shown in Figure 6.2.

The general public can book rooms at any of the chain's hotels by:

- Contacting staff in the hotel, who then use a GUI front-end to make the booking.
- Telephoning customer services who then use a GUI front-end to make the booking.
- Using the company's website to make the booking online.

In all cases, communication with the mainframe computer is done via a middleware layer of XML messages.

There is a document production system that produces paper and electronic versions of customer correspondence such as booking confirmations, bills, invoices, etc.

Direct debit and credit card payments are made via BACS. Files are transmitted and confirmation and error messages are received back.

Validation of bank account details is performed by sending XML messages to and from a third-party system.

Validation and enquiry of address and postcode is also performed by sending XML messages to and from a third-party system.

A new release of the system is planned for six months' time. This will include:

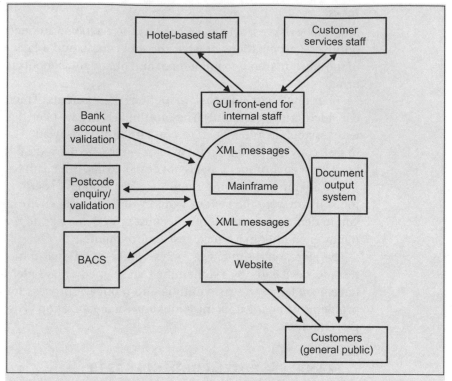

FIGURE 6.2 *Hotel system architecture*

- Code changes to improve performance in the XML middleware layer and on the mainframe. Mainframe changes will be performed by an outsourced development team in India.

- Various changes to website screens to improve usability.

- The introduction of a new third-party calendar object from which dates can be selected.

- The ability for customers to pay by cheque.

- The automatic production of cheques for refunds, cancellations, etc.

- An amended customer bill plus two other amended documents.

- Two new output documents.

- Fixes to various existing low- and medium-severity defects.

CHECK OF UNDERSTANDING

(1) Would you expect a quick return on your investment in test tools? Why?

(2) Describe three potential benefits of using test tools.

(3) Describe two risks of using test tools.

TEST TOOLS

Types of tool

There are several ways in which test tools can be classified. They can be classified according to:

- the part of the fundamental test process with which they are primarily associated;
- the type of testing that they support;
- who uses them.

In this book, test tools will be classified according to the type of activity they support (as in the ISTQB Foundation Level Syllabus, version 2005, 1/7/2005).

Tool support for management of testing and tests

Test management tools

Test management tools provide support for various activities and tasks throughout the development life cycle. Some of these activities are supported by the provision of interfaces to other more specialist tools (for instance, test execution tools). Other test management tools provide fully integrated modules that provide some or all of the services/functions provided by more specialist tools (such as incident management or requirements management tools).

The diagram in Figure 6.3 shows how a test management tool is the hub or centre of a set of integrated test tools.

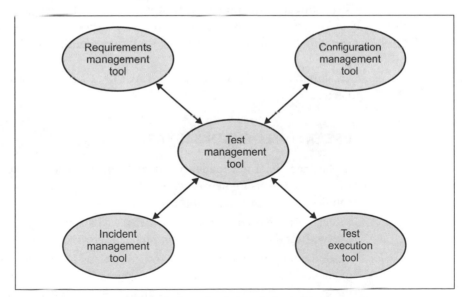

FIGURE 6.3 *An integrated set of tools*

Test management tools provide a framework for creating, storing and editing test procedures. These may be linked or traced to requirements, test conditions and risks. Such test procedures can then be prioritized or grouped together and scheduled so that they are run in the most effective and efficient order. Some test management tools allow dependencies to be recorded so that tests that will fail owing to a known defect can be highlighted and left unexecuted. This allows testers to be redirected to run the highest priority tests available rather than waste their time and the test data they have prepared on tests that are certain to fail.

Tests can be recorded as passed or failed and usually a test management tool provides an interface to an incident management tool so that an incident can be raised if the actual and expected results differ.

Test management tools can provide management information and reports on test procedures passed or failed. The amount of integration with other specialist tools is significant here. For instance, integration with requirements management tools allows reports to be produced on test progress against one or more requirements. Integration with incident management tools allows reports also to include analysis of defects against requirements.

Test management tools generally hold data in a database. This allows a large amount of reports and metrics to be produced. The metrics produced can be used as inputs to:

- Test and project management to control the current project.
- Estimates for future projects.
- Identifying weaknesses or inefficiencies in the development or test process that can be subsequently investigated with the aim of improving them.

Test management information reports should be designed to meet the needs of project managers and other key users. It may be necessary to export data to a spreadsheet in order for it to be manipulated into the format required.

A test management tool can enable reuse of existing testware in future test projects.

USE IN HOTEL CHAIN SCENARIO

In the scenario, a test management tool can be used to write down and store requirements for new functionality and subsequently to hold the test conditions necessary to test these requirements.

It can also be used to record whether tests have passed or failed and to produce test management information on progress to date.

Additionally, requirements and test conditions from previous developments will already exist in the test management tool. These can be used as the basis for the regression testing required. Indeed a regression pack may already exist. Clearly the regression pack would have to be reviewed and amended as necessary to make it relevant to this release. However, the benefit is that much of the previous work could be reused which, in turn, means that much less effort will be involved to create a regression pack.

Incident management tools

Incident management tools (also known as defect management tools) are one of the most widely used types of test tool. At a basic level incident management tools are used to provide two critical activities: creation of an incident report; and maintenance of details about the incident as it progresses through the incident life cycle.

The level of detail to be captured about the incident can be varied depending upon the characteristics of the tool itself and the way in which the incident management tool is configured and used by the test organization.

For example, the incident management tool could be configured so that lots of mandatory information is required in order to comply with industry or generic standards such as IEEE 1044. In addition, workflow rules may also be applied to ensure that the agreed incident life cycle is strictly applied, with incidents only able to be assigned to particular teams or users. Alternatively, the tool could be configured to require very limited mandatory information, with most fields being free format.

Incident management tools also use a database to store and manage details of incidents. This allows the incident to be categorized according to the values stored in appropriate fields. Such values will change during the incident life cycle as the incident is analysed, debugged, fixed and confirmation tested. It is often possible to view the history of changes made to the incident.

The database structure also enables incidents to be searched and analysed (using either filters or more complex SQL-type queries). This provides the basis for management information about incidents. Note that as the values held against each incident change, the management information will also change. Therefore users need to be aware of the danger of using outdated reports.

This data can also be used in conjunction with data held in test management tools when planning and estimating for future projects. It can also be analysed to provide input to test process improvement projects.

Fields in the database structure normally include:

- Priority (e.g. high, medium, low).
- Severity (e.g. high, medium, low).
- Assignee (the person to whom the incident is currently assigned, e.g. a developer for debugging, a tester to perform confirmation testing).
- Status in the incident life cycle (e.g. New, Open, Fixed, Reopen, Closed).

This would allow management information to be produced from the incident management database about the number of high-priority incidents with a status of Open or Reopen that are assigned to Peter Morgan, compared with the number assigned to Brian Hambling.

Some test management tools include fully integrated incident management tools as part of their core product, whilst other incident management tools can be integrated with test management, requirements management and/or test execution tools. Such integration enables incidents to be input and related to test cases and requirements.

USE IN HOTEL CHAIN SCENARIO

An incident management tool can be used to raise new defects and process them through the defect life cycle until resolved. It can also be used to check whether defects (or similar defects) have been raised before, especially for defects raised during regression testing.

An incident management tool could also be used to prioritize defects so that developers fix the most important ones first. It could also highlight clusters of defects. This may suggest that more detailed testing needs to be done on the areas of functionality where most defects are being found as it is probable that further defects will be found as well.

Requirements management tools

Requirements management tools are used by business analysts to record, manage and prioritize the requirements of a system. They can also be used to manage changes to requirements – something that can be a significant problem for testers as test cases are designed and executed to establish whether the delivered system meets its requirements. Therefore if requirements change after tests have been written then test cases may also need to change. There is also a potential problem of changes not being communicated to all interested parties, thus testers could be using an old set of requirements whilst new ones are being issued to developers.

The use of a traceability function within a requirements tool (and/or integrated with a test management tool) enables links and references to be made between requirements, functions, test conditions and other testware items. This means that as requirements change, it is easy to identify which other items may need to change.

Some requirements management tools can be integrated with test management tools, whilst some test management tools enable requirements to be input and related to test cases.

Requirements management tools also enable requirements coverage metrics to be calculated easily as traceability enables test cases to be mapped to requirements.

As can be seen, traceability can create a lot of maintenance work, but it does highlight those areas that are undergoing change.

USE IN HOTEL CHAIN SCENARIO

A change is required to three documents sent to customers. The requirements are documented in the requirements management tool. Testers obtain the requirements from the tool and begin to devise test conditions and test cases. A subsequent change control means that further changes are made to the requirements. The testers should be made aware of the changes so that they can provide input to the impact analysis. However, traceability within a requirements tool will also highlight the test conditions affected by the changed requirement. The testers can review the change in requirements and then consider what changes need to be made to the test conditions and test cases.

Configuration management tools

Configuration management tools are designed primarily for managing: the versions of different software (and hardware) components that comprise a complete build of the system; and various complete builds of systems that exist for various software platforms over a period of time.

A build is a development activity where a complete system is compiled and linked (typically daily) so that a consistent system is available at any time including all latest changes.

USE IN HOTEL CHAIN SCENARIO

Within the hotel booking system, there will be many versions of subsystems due to the date at which the version was included in a build, or the operating system on which the version works, etc. Each version of a subsystem will have a unique version number and each version of a subsystem will comprise many different components (e.g. program files, data files, DLLs, etc.).

The configuration management tool maps the version number of each subsystem to the build (or release) number of the integrated system. As shown in Table 6.1, Build A (UNIX) and Build B (Microsoft Windows 2003) might use the same version (v1.02) of the Payments Out subsystem, but Release C might use version v1.04.

TABLE 6.1 *Configuration traceability*

Build for integrated system	Version of Payments Out system	Cheque test procedure ID	Check BACS file test procedure ID
Build A	v1.02	TP123a	TP201
Build B	v1.02	TP123b	TP201
Build C	v1.04	TP123b	TP201

The same principle applies to testware with a different version number for a test procedure being used, depending upon the version number of the build. For instance, test procedure TP123a might be used for Build A and TP123b might be used for Build B – even though both have the same purpose and even expected results. However, another test procedure, TP201, may be applicable to all builds.

The amount of benefit to be obtained from using configuration management tools is largely dependent upon:

- the complexity of the system architecture;
- the number and frequency of builds of the integrated system;
- how much choice (options) are available to customers (whether internal or external).

For example, a software house selling different versions of a product to many customers who run on a variety of operating systems is likely to find configuration management tools more useful than an internal development department working on a single operating system for a single customer.

The use of configuration management tools allows traceability between testware and builds of an integrated system and versions of subsystems and modules. Traceability is useful for:

- identifying the correct version of test procedures to be used;
- determining which test procedures and other testware can be reused or need to be updated/maintained;
- assisting the debugging process so that a failure found when running a test procedure can be traced back to the appropriate version of a subsystem.

CHECK OF UNDERSTANDING

(1) What is traceability?

(2) Which tool is likely to be most closely integrated with a requirements management tool?

(3) Which tool would you use to identify the version of the software component being tested?

Tool support for static testing

Review process support tools

Review process support tools provide a framework for reviews or inspections. This can include:

- Maintaining information about the review process, such as rules and checklists.
- The ability to record, communicate and retain review comments and defects.
- The ability to amend and reissue the deliverable under review whilst retaining a history or log of the changes made.

- Traceability functions to enable changes to deliverables under review to highlight other deliverables that may be affected by the change.
- The use of web technology to provide access from any geographical location to this information.

Review process support tools can interface with configuration management tools to control the version numbers of a document under review.

If reviews and inspections are already performed effectively then such a review process support tool can be implemented fairly quickly and relatively cheaply. However, if such a tool is used as a means for imposing the use of reviews then the training and implementation costs will be fairly high (as would be the case for implementing a review process without such tools). These tools support the review process, but management buy-in to reviews is necessary if benefits from using such tools are to be obtained in the long run.

These tools tend to be more beneficial for peer (or technical) reviews and inspections rather than walkthroughs and informal reviews.

USE IN HOTEL CHAIN SCENARIO

The hotel company could use a review process support tool to perform a review of a system specification written in the UK, so that offshore developers can be involved in the review process. In turn, the review of program code, written offshore, could also be performed using such a tool. This means that both the UK and offshore staff could be involved in both reviews, with no excuses for the right people not being available to attend.

Static analysis tools

Static analysis tools enable developers to analyse code before it is executed in order to identify defects as early as possible. The static analysis tool generates lots of error and warning messages about the code. Training may be required in order to interpret these messages and it may also be necessary to configure the tool to filter out particular types of warning messages that are not relevant. The use of static analysis tools on existing or amended code is likely to result in lots of messages concerning programming standards. A way of dealing with this situation should be considered during the selection and implementation process. For instance, it may be agreed that small changes to existing code should not use the static analysis tool and medium to large changes to existing code should use the static analysis tool. A rewrite should be considered if the existing code is significantly non-compliant.

Static analysis tools can find defects that are hard to find during dynamic testing. They can also be used to improve the understanding of the code and to calculate complexity and other metrics (see Chapter 3).

Some static analysis tools are integrated with dynamic analysis tools and coverage measurement tools. They are usually language specific, so to test code written in C++ you would need to have a version of a static analysis tool that was specific to C++.

Other static analysis tools come as part of programming languages or only work with particular development platforms. Note that debugging tools and compilers provide some basic functions of a static analysis tool, but they are generally not considered to be test tools and are excluded from the ISTQB syllabus.

The types of defect that can be found using a static analysis tool can include:

- Syntax errors (e.g. spelling or missing punctuation).
- Variance from programming standards (e.g. too difficult to maintain).
- Invalid code structures (missing ENDIF statements).
- The structure of the code means that some modules or sections of code may not be executed. Such unreachable code or invalid code dependencies may point to errors in code structure.
- Portability (e.g. code compiles on Windows but not on UNIX).
- Security vulnerabilities.
- Inconsistent interfaces between components (e.g. XML messages produced by component A are not of the correct format to be read by component B).
- References to variables that have a null value or variables declared but never used.

USE IN HOTEL CHAIN SCENARIO

Static analysis tools may be considered worthwhile for code being developed by offshore development teams who are not familiar with in-house coding standards. Such tools may also be considered beneficial for high-risk functions such as BACS and other external interfaces.

Modelling tools

Modelling tools are used primarily by developers during the analysis and design stages of the development life cycle. The reason modelling tools are included here is because they are very cost effective at finding defects early in the development life cycle.

Their benefits are similar to those obtained from the use of reviews and inspections, in that modelling tools allow omissions and inconsistencies to be identified and fixed early so that detailed design and programming can begin from a consistent and robust model. This in turn prevents fault multiplication that can occur if developers build from the wrong model.

For instance, a visual modelling tool using UML can be used by designers to build a model of the software specification. The tool can map business processes to the system architecture model, which, in turn, enables programmers and testers to have a better and common understanding of what programs should do and what testing is required.

Similarly, the use of database, state or object models can help to identify what testing is required and can assist in checking whether tests cover all necessary transactions.

USE IN HOTEL CHAIN SCENARIO

The modelling tool could help to identify missing scenarios from letter templates or the need to update letters with new paragraphs. Again, the benefits of a clearly defined, consistent model of the software will assist offshore companies to develop software that meets the requirements of the customer.

The use of modelling tools is particularly useful in complex system architectures such as in this scenario.

CHECK OF UNDERSTANDING

(1) Which of the tools used for static testing is/are most likely to be used by developers rather than testers?

(2) In which part of the fundamental test process are static analysis tools likely to be most useful?

(3) What is a significant benefit of using modelling tools from a testing perspective?

Tool support for test specification

Test design tools

Test design tools are used to support the generation and creation of test cases. In order for the tool to generate test cases, a test basis needs to be input and maintained. Therefore many test design tools are integrated with other tools that already contain details of the test basis such as:

- modelling tools;
- requirements management tools;
- static analysis tools;
- test management tools.

The level of automation can vary and depends upon the characteristics of the tool itself and the way in which the test basis is recorded in the tool. For example, some tools allow specifications or requirements to be specified in a formal language. This can allow test cases with inputs and expected results to be generated. Other test design tools allow a GUI model of the test basis to be created and then allow tests to be generated from this model.

Other tools (sometimes known as test frames) merely generate a partly filled template from the requirement specification held in narrative form. The tester will then need to add to the template and copy and edit as necessary to create the test cases required.

Tests designed from database, object or state models held in modelling tools can be used to verify that the model has been built correctly and can be used to derive some test cases. Tests derived can be very thorough and give high levels of coverage in certain areas.

Some static analysis tools integrate with tools that generate test cases from an analysis of the code. These can include test input values and expected results.

A test oracle is a type of test design tool that automatically generates expected results. However, these are rarely available as they perform the same function as the software under test. They tend to be available for:

- Replacement systems
- Migrations
- Regression testing

USE IN HOTEL CHAIN SCENARIO

A test oracle could be built using a spreadsheet to support the testing of customers' bills. The tester can then input details for calculating bills such as the total bill based on various transaction types, refunds, VAT, etc. The spreadsheet could then calculate the total bill amount and this should match the bill calculated by the system under test.

However, test design tools should be only part of the approach to test design. They need to be supplemented by other test cases designed with the use of other techniques and the application of risk.

Test design tools could be used by the test organization in the scenario but the overhead to import the necessary data from the test basis may be too great to give any real overall benefit. However, if the test design tool can import requirements or other aspects of the test basis easily then it may become worthwhile.

Test design tools tend to be more useful for safety-critical and other high-risk software when coverage levels are higher and industry, defence or government standards need to be adhered to. Generally commercial software applications, such as the hotel system, do not require such high standards and therefore test design tools are of less benefit in such cases.

Test data preparation tools

Test data preparation tools are typically used by developers to manipulate data so that the environment is in the appropriate state for the test to be run. This can involve making changes to the field values in databases, data files, etc., and populating files with a spread of data, including dates of birth, names from a centrally held repository, etc.

USE IN HOTEL CHAIN SCENARIO

A set of test data may be created by taking, say, 5 per cent of all records from the live system and scrambling personal details so that data is protected and to ensure that customer letters being tested are not wrongly sent to real customers. Data could be taken from the mainframe system, but it is also very important to retain integrity of data between different systems. Data that is held in other databases would need to remain consistent with records on the mainframe.

The knowledge of the database structure and which fields need to be de-personalized is likely to lie with the development team – so it is important to consider whether to buy a tool or build it within the organization.

CHECK OF UNDERSTANDING

(1) What is the main difference and similarity between a test frame and a test oracle?

(2) What types of inputs can a test design tool use to generate test cases?

(3) Which test specification tool is generally used by developers?

Tool support for test execution and logging

Test comparators

Test comparators compare the contents of files, databases, XML messages, objects and other electronic data formats. This allows expected results and actual results to be compared. They can also highlight differences and thus provide assistance to developers when localizing and debugging code.

They often have functions that allow specified sections of the file, screen or object to be ignored or masked out. This means that a date or time stamp on a screen or field can be masked out as it is expected to be different when a comparison is performed.

Table 6.2 shows an extract from the transaction table in the hotel chain database for data created on 20/10/2006.

TABLE 6.2   *Hotel system extract (20/10/2006)*

Transaction ID	Trans_Date	Amount _exc_VAT	VAT	CustomerID
12345	20/10/2006	359.66	62.94	AG0012
12346	20/10/2006	2312.01	404.60	HJ0007

A regression test was run on 5/11/2006. Table 6.3 shows an extract from the transaction table for this data.

TABLE 6.3   *Hotel system extract (5/11/2006)*

Transaction ID	Trans_Date	Amount _exc_VAT	VAT	CustomerID
12369	5/11/2006	359.66	62.94	AG0012
12370	5/11/2006	2312.01	404.60	HJ0007

The Transaction ID and Trans_Date fields contain different values. But we know why this is the case and we would expect them to be different. Therefore we can mask out these values. Note that some test comparators may provide functions to add on values to take into account known differences (e.g. 15 days later) so that the actual results and expected results can be compared.

Comparators are particularly useful for regression testing since the contents of output or interface files should usually be the same. This is probably the test tool that provides the single greatest benefit. For instance, manually comparing the contents of a database query containing thousands of rows is time consuming, error prone and demotivating. The same task can be performed accurately and in a fraction of the time using a comparator. Comparators are usually included in test execution tools.

Test execution tools

Test execution tools allow test scripts to be run automatically (or at least semi-automatically). A test script (written in a programming language or scripting language) is used to navigate through the system under test and to compare predefined expected outcomes with actual outcomes. The results of the test run are written to a test log. Test scripts can then be amended and reused to run different scenarios through the same system.

Record (or capture playback) tools: Record (or capture playback) tools can be used to record a test script and then play it back exactly as it was executed. However, a test script usually fails when played back owing to unexpected results or unrecognized objects. This may sound surprising but consider entering a new customer record onto a system:

- When the script was recorded, the customer record did not exist. When the script is played back the system correctly recognizes that this customer record already exists and produces a different response, thus causing the test script to fail.

- When a test script is played back and actual and expected results are compared a date or time may be displayed. The comparison facility will spot this difference and report a failure.

- Other problems include the inability of test execution tools to recognize some types of GUI control or object. This might be able to be resolved by coding or reconfiguring the object characteristics (but this can be quite complicated and should be left to experts in the tool).

The recording of tests can be useful during exploratory testing for reproducing a defect or for documenting how to execute a test. In addition, such tools can be used to capture user actions so that the navigation through a system can be recorded. In both cases, the script can then be made more robust by a technical expert so that it handles valid system behaviours depending upon the inputs and the state of the system under test.

Data-driven testing: Robust test scripts that deal with various inputs can be converted into data-driven tests. This is where hard-coded inputs in the test script are replaced with variables that point to data in a data-table. Data-tables are usually spreadsheets with one test case per row, with each row containing test inputs and expected results. The test script reads the appropriate data value from the data-table and inserts it at the appropriate point in the script (e.g. the value in the Customer Name column is inserted into the Customer Name field on the input screen).

Keyword-driven testing: A further enhancement to data-driven testing is the use of keyword-driven (or action word) testing. Keywords are included as extra columns in the data-table. The script reads the keyword and takes the appropriate actions and subsequent path through the system under test. Conditional programming constructs such as IF ELSE statements or SELECT CASE statements are required in the test script for keyword-driven testing.

Technical skills: Programming skills and programming standards are required to use the tool effectively. It may be that these can be provided by a small team of technical experts within the test organization or from an external company. In data-driven and particularly keyword-driven approaches, the bulk of the work can be done by manual testers defining their test cases and test data and then running their tests and raising defects as required. However, this relies on robust and well-written test scripts that are easy to maintain. This takes much time and effort before any sort of payback is achieved.

Maintenance: It is essential that time (and subsequent budget) is allowed for test scripts to be maintained. Any change to a system can mean that the test scripts need to be updated. Therefore, the introduction of a new type of object or control could result in a mismatch being found between the previous object type and the new one. The relevant level of technical skills and knowledge is also required to do this.

Effective and efficient use: The efficiency and effectiveness benefits that come from the use of a test execution tool take a long time to come to fruition. First, the selection and implementation process needs to be planned and conducted effectively (a generic process for selecting and implementing any type of test tool is detailed later in this chapter). However, there are certain issues that are particularly relevant to test execution tools and these are described below.

The long-term benefits of test execution tools include:

- Cost savings as a result of the time saved by running automated tests rather than manual tests.
- Accuracy benefits from avoiding manual errors in execution and comparison.

- The ability and flexibility to use skilled testers on more useful and interesting tasks (than running repetitive manual tests).
- The speed with which the results of the regression pack can be obtained.

Note that benefits come primarily from running the same or very similar tests a number of times on a stable platform. Therefore they are generally most useful for regression testing.

USE IN HOTEL CHAIN SCENARIO

Let us assume that a test execution tool is already used for regression testing. Existing automated test scripts could be analysed to identify which ones can be reused and to identify gaps in the coverage for the new enhancement. These gaps could be filled by running cases manually or by writing new automated test scripts. Rather than starting from scratch, it may be possible to produce additional automated scripts by reusing some code or modules already used by existing scripts.

In this enhancement, the automated scripts used to test the unchanged documents could be run without having to be amended.

The automated scripts to produce the amended documents would need to be analysed and updated as required. The navigation part of the script would be largely unchanged but the comparison between actual and expected results would probably be performed manually the first time round. Once the test has passed manually, the comparison could be added to the script for reuse in the future.

Automated scripts for new documents could be added to the regression pack after this release is complete.

The graph in Figure 6.4 shows how the benefits of using test execution tools take some time to pay back. Note how in the early stages the cost of using automated regression testing is greater than the cost of manual regression testing. This is due to the initial investment, implementation, training, initial development of automated scripts, etc. However, the cost each additional time the test is run is less for automated regression testing than it is for manual regression testing. Therefore the lines on the graph converge and at a point in time (known as the break-even point) the lines cross. This is the point at which the total cost to date for automated testing is less than the total cost to date for manual regression testing.

This is clearly a simplistic view but it demonstrates how an initial investment in test execution tools can be of financial benefit in the medium to long term. There are other less tangible benefits as well. However, to get this financial benefit you will need to be sure that there is a requirement to run the same (or very similar) regression tests on many occasions.

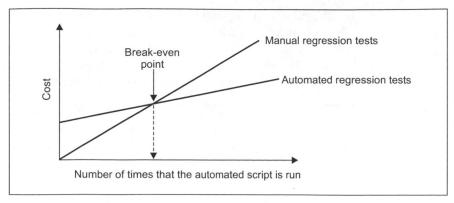

FIGURE 6.4 *Test execution tools payback model*

Test harnesses

Test harnesses (also known as unit test framework tools) are used primarily by developers to simulate a small section of the environment in which the software will operate. They are usually written in-house by developers to perform component or integration testing for a specific purpose.

Test harnesses can be used to test various systems or objects ranging from a middleware system (as in Figure 6.5) to a single or small group of components.

USE IN HOTEL CHAIN SCENARIO

Bookings are entered via the web or GUI front-ends and are loaded onto the mainframe. An overnight batch runs on the mainframe and generates XML messages that are then processed by the middleware system, which makes a further call to the mainframe to read other data. The middleware system then generates further XML messages, which are processed by other systems, resulting in the production of letters to customers.

There are several benefits that can be obtained from using a test harness that generates the XML messages produced by the mainframe:

- It would take a lot of time and effort to design and execute test cases on the mainframe system and run the batch.

- It would be costly to build a full environment.

- The mainframe code needed to generate the XML messages may not yet be available.

- A smaller environment is easier to control and manage. It enables developers (or testers) to perform component and integration testing more quickly as it is easier to localize defects. This allows a quicker turn-round time for fixing defects.

The diagram in Figure 6.5 shows that a test harness has been built (e.g. using a spreadsheet and macros) to generate XML messages and send them to the middleware. A stub is used to simulate the calls made by the middleware to the mainframe. The contents of the XML messages produced by the middleware can then be compared with the expected results.

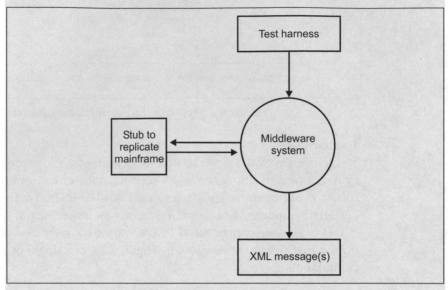

FIGURE 6.5   *Test harness for middleware*

There are similarities with the principle behind data-driven testing using test execution tools, as the harness allows many different test cases to be designed and run without the time-consuming process of keying them manually. This raises the question of how much benefit can be obtained from using a test execution tool when a test harness can be used instead. As usual, it depends on the circumstances, the risk, the purpose and the level of testing being performed.

Coverage measurement tools
Coverage measurement tools measure the percentage of the code structure covered across white-box measurement techniques such as statement coverage and branch or decision coverage. In addition, they can also be used to measure coverage of modules and function calls. Coverage measurement tools are often integrated with static and dynamic analysis tools and are primarily used by developers.

Coverage measurement tools can measure code written in several programming languages, but not all tools can measure code written in all languages. They are useful for reporting coverage measurement and can therefore be used to assess test completion criteria and/or exit criteria.

Coverage measurement of requirements and test cases/scripts run can usually be obtained from test management tools. This function is unlikely to be provided by coverage measurement tools.

Coverage measurement is performed by instrumenting the code with extra statements. The code is then executed and the extra statements write back to a log in order to identify which statements and branches have been executed. Instrumentation code can then be removed before it goes into production.

USE IN HOTEL CHAIN SCENARIO

Coverage measurement tools are generally used on high risk and safety critical systems and therefore would probably not be used in the Hotel Chain Scenario. However, as an example, assume that the exit criteria for a test phase include the criteria shown in Table 6.4.

TABLE 6.4 *Exit criteria*

Function	Module risk level	Branch coverage	Statement coverage
BACS	High	100%	100%
Mailshot	Medium	Not specified	100%
Look-up error message/screen navigation	Low	50%	75%

In this case, coverage measurement tools would be the most appropriate method of assessing whether the exit criteria have been met.

Security tools

Security testing tools are used to test the functions that detect security threats. The security testing tool would typically support the execution of test procedures to confirm that computer viruses, denial of service attacks or any other specified attacks are handled as required.

Security testing tools are mainly used to test e-commerce, e-business and websites. For example, a third-party security application such as a firewall may be integrated into a web-based application.

The skills required to use security tools are very specialized. Therefore it may be worth considering the use of specialist consultancies to perform such testing.

Security tools need to be constantly updated, as there are problems solved and new vulnerabilities discovered all the time – consider the number of Windows XP security releases to see the scale of security problems.

USE IN HOTEL CHAIN SCENARIO

Security tools could be used to test that the firewall surrounding the website can prevent disruption from any type of attack that is specified within the security tool.

In addition, encryption of XML messages to validate bank account details could be tested.

CHECK OF UNDERSTANDING

(1) Why is implementing a comparator likely to be cheaper and quicker than implementing a test execution tool?

(2) Why is the use of test execution tools for record and playback not as effective as it may sound?

(3) Are test execution tools likely to be more useful for testing new systems or testing changes to existing systems? Explain why.

(4) Would both a test execution tool and a test harness be appropriate for acceptance testing?

(5) Name three potential benefits from implementing a test execution tool.

(6) Give three reasons why a test harness is an efficient way of testing components.

(7) Which test execution and logging tools are typically used by developers?

(8) Which test execution and logging tools are likely to be used by specialists in the use of that tool?

Tool support for performance and monitoring

Dynamic analysis tools

Dynamic analysis tools are used to detect the type of defects that are difficult to find during static testing. They are typically used by developers, during component testing and component integration testing, to:

- report on the state of software during its execution;
- monitor the allocation, use and deallocation of memory;
- identify memory leaks;
- detect time dependencies;
- identify unassigned pointers;
- check pointer arithmetic.

They are generally used for safety-critical and other high-risk software where reliability is critical.

Dynamic analysis tools are often integrated with static analysis and coverage measurement tools. For example, a developer may want to perform static analysis on code to localize defects so that they can be removed before component test execution. The integrated tool may allow:

- the code to be analysed statically;
- the code to be instrumented;
- the code to be executed (dynamically).

Dynamic analysis tools are usually language specific, so to test code written in C++ you would need to have a version of a dynamic analysis tool that was specific to C++.

The tool could then:

- report static defects;
- report dynamic defects;
- provide coverage measurement figures;
- report upon the code being (dynamically) executed at various instrumentation points.

USE IN HOTEL CHAIN SCENARIO

The hotel chain would probably not use dynamic analysis tools as the benefits for a normal commercial software system (such as this) are relatively small compared with the investment and on-going costs of dynamic testing tools. However, if static analysis and coverage measurement tools are used then the additional cost of using dynamic analysis tools may be reduced as they usually come in the same package. Another contributory factor in the decision is that the work done during static analysis and coverage measurement may mean that little additional effort is required to run dynamic tests.

Performance testing/load testing/stress testing tools

Performance testing is very difficult to do accurately and in a repeatable way without using test tools. Therefore performance testing tools have been developed to carry out both load testing and stress testing.

Load testing reports upon the performance of a system under test, under various loads and usage patterns. A test driver can be used to simulate the load or usage pattern. Alternatively, response times or transaction times can be measured under various levels of usage by running automated repetitive test scripts via the user interface of the system under test. In both cases output will be written to a log. Reports or graphs can be generated from the contents of the log to monitor the level of performance.

Performance testing tools can also be used for stress testing. In this case, the load on the system under test is increased gradually in order to identify the usage pattern or load at which the system under test fails. For example, if an air traffic control system supports 200 concurrent aircraft in the defined air space, the entry of the 201st or 205th aircraft should not cause the whole system to fail.

Performance testing tools can be used against whole systems but they can also be used during system integration test to test an integrated group of systems, one or more servers, one or more databases or a whole environment.

If the risk analysis finds that the likelihood of performance degradation is low then it is likely that no performance testing will be carried out. For instance, a small enhancement to an existing mainframe system would not necessarily require any formal performance testing. Normal manual testing may be considered sufficient (during which poor performance might be noticed).

There are similarities between performance testing tools and test execution tools in that they both use test scripts and data-driven testing. They can both be left to run unattended overnight and both need a heavy upfront investment which will take some period of time to pay back.

Performance testing tools can find defects such as:

- General performance problems.
- Performance bottlenecks.
- Memory leakage (e.g. if the system is left running under heavy load for some time).
- Record-locking problems.
- Concurrency problems.
- Excess usage of system resources.
- Exhaustion of disk space.

The cost of some performance tools is high and the implementation and training costs are also high. In addition, finding experts in performance testing is not that easy. Therefore it is worth considering using specialist consultancies to come in and carry out performance testing using such tools.

USE IN HOTEL CHAIN SCENARIO

The likelihood of poor website performance and the cost of lost business and reputation are likely to be sufficient to justify the use of performance testing to mitigate this risk. Performance testing can range from using a relatively cheap tool to indicate whether performance has improved or deteriorated as a result of the enhancement to an extensive assessment of response times under normal or maximum predicted usage and identification of the usage pattern that will cause the system to fail.

It is likely that performance test tools will have been used when the website was first developed. Therefore it may be easy to reuse existing tools to do a regression test of performance. If performance tools were not used when the website was developed it is unlikely to be worthwhile buying and implementing expensive performance testing tools.

> An alternative option would be to use tools that already exist on servers or in the test environment to monitor performance. It may also be worth considering using external consultants.

Monitoring tools

Monitoring tools are used to check whether systems are available and whether their performance is acceptable. Such tools are mainly used in live rather than test environments and are therefore not really testing tools. They tend to be used for monitoring e-commerce, e-business or websites as such systems are more likely to be affected by factors external to the organization and the consequences can be severe in terms of business lost and bad publicity. Generally, if a website is not available, customers will not report it but will go elsewhere. For example, it was reported in 2003 that a well-known online retailer would lose sales of $660,000 per hour if it were offline during the US trading day.

The use of monitoring tools is generally less important for internal systems as failure is more likely to be noticed only within the organization and contingency plans may also exist.

USE IN HOTEL CHAIN SCENARIO

A monitoring tool may be beneficial to monitor the website. A monitoring tool may also exist as part of the mainframe system. However, it is less likely that monitoring tools will be used for the GUI front-end that is used by internal staff.

CHECK OF UNDERSTANDING

(1) Describe two types of defect that can typically be found using dynamic analysis tools.

(2) Describe two drawbacks associated with performance testing tools.

(3) Which of the tools that provide support for performance and monitoring is most likely to be used by developers?

Other tools

Other tools that are not designed specifically for testers or developers can also be used to support one or more test activities. These include:

- Spreadsheets
- Word processors
- E-mail
- Back-up and restore utilities
- SQL and other database query tools

- Project planning tools
- Debugging tools.

For example, in the absence of test management or incident management tools, defects could be recorded on word processors and could be tracked and maintained on spreadsheets. Tests passed or failed could also be recorded on spreadsheets.

USE IN HOTEL CHAIN SCENARIO

Other software tools could also be used:

- A spreadsheet could be used for producing decision tables or working out all the different test scenarios required. It could also be used to manipulate test management information so that it can be presented in the format required in weekly or daily test progress reports.
- Word processors could be used for writing test strategies, test plans, weekly reports and other test deliverables.
- E-mail could be used for communicating with developers about defects and for distributing test reports and other deliverables.
- Back-up and restore utilities could be used to restore a consistent set of data into the test environment for regression testing.
- SQL could be used for analysing the data held in databases in order to obtain actual or expected results.
- Project planning tools could be used to estimate resources and timescales and monitor progress.
- Debugging tools can be used by developers to localize and fix defects.

CHECK OF UNDERSTANDING

Name four tools that are not specifically designed for testers. Give an example of how each of them could be of use to a tester.

Summary of test tools

Table 6.5 summarizes the types of test tools discussed above. It includes the definition given in the ISTQB Glossary of Testing Terms v1.1 and gives a guide to:

- the main ISTQB syllabus classification;
- the activity in the fundamental test process for which the tool is usually most useful;
- the most likely users of the tool.

TABLE 6.5 *Types of test tool*

Tool type	ISTQB Syllabus classification	Activity in fundamental test process where it is usually most beneficial	ISTQB Glossary of Testing Terms definition	Most likely users
Test management tool	Management of testing and tests	All activities	A tool that provides support to the test management and control part of a test process. It often has several capabilities, such as testware management, scheduling of tests, the logging of results, progress tracking, incident management and test reporting.	Testers
Incident management tool	Management of testing and tests	Implementation and execution	A tool that facilitates the recording and status tracking of defects. These tools often have workflow-oriented facilities to track and control the allocation, correction and retesting of defects and provide reporting facilities. Also known as defect-tracking tools.	Various, but particularly testers
Requirements management tool	Management of testing and tests	Analysis and design	A tool that supports the recording of requirements, requirements attributes (e.g. priority, knowledge responsible) and annotation, and facilitates traceability through layers of requirements and requirements change management. Some requirements management tools also provide facilities for static analysis, such as consistency checking and violations to predefined requirements rules.	Various, but particularly business analysts
Configuration management tool	Management of testing and tests	Implementation and execution	Not defined	Various
Review process support tool	Static testing	Implementation and execution	A tool that provides support to the review process. Typical features include review planning and tracking support, communication support, collaborative reviews and a repository for collecting and reporting of metrics.	Various
Static analysis tools	Static testing	Implementation and execution	Performs and supports analysis of software artifacts, e.g. requirements or code, carried out without execution of these software artifacts.	Developers
Modelling tools	Static testing	Implementation and execution	Not defined.	Developers
Test design tools/script generators	Test specification	Analysis and design	A tool that supports the test design activity by generating test inputs from a specification that may be held in a CASE tool repository, e.g. requirements management tool, or from specified test conditions held in the tool itself.	Testers
Test oracles (considered to be a subset of test design tools	Test specification	Analysis and design	A source to determine expected results to compare with the actual result of the software under test. An oracle may be the existing system (for a benchmark), a user manual, or an individual's specialized knowledge, but should not be the code.	Testers
Test (input) data preparation tools	Test specification	Analysis and design	A type of test tool that enables data to be selected from existing databases or created, generated, manipulated and edited for use in testing.	Developers
Test execution/test running tools	Test execution and logging	Implementation and execution	A type of test tool that is able to execute other software using an automated test script, e.g. capture/playback.	Testers

Tool type	ISTQB Syllabus classification	Activity in fundamental test process where it is usually most beneficial	ISTQB Glossary of Testing Terms definition	Most likely users
Test harness/unit test framework tools (stubs and drivers)	Test execution and logging	Implementation and execution	A test environment composed of stubs and drivers needed to conduct a test.	Developers
Test comparators	Test execution and logging	Implementation and execution	A test tool used to support and/or automate the process of identifying differences between the actual results produced by the component or system under test and the expected results for a test. Test comparison can be performed during test execution (dynamic comparison) or after test execution.	Testers and developers
Coverage measurement tools	Test execution and logging	Implementation and execution	A tool that provides objective measures of what structural elements, e.g. statements, branches, have been exercised by a test suite.	Developers
Security tools	Test execution and logging	Implementation and execution	A tool that supports testing to determine the security of the software product. Security is defined as: attributes of software products that bear on its ability to prevent unauthorized access, whether accidental or deliberate, to programs and data.	Security testing specialists
Dynamic analysis tools	Performance and monitoring	Implementation and execution	A tool that provides run-time information on the state of the software code. These tools are most commonly used to identify unassigned pointers, check pointer arithmetic and to monitor the allocation, use and deallocation of memory and to flag memory leaks.	Developers
Performance testing/load testing/stress testing tools	Performance and monitoring	Implementation and execution	A tool to support performance testing and that usually has two main facilities: load generation and test transaction measurement. Load generation can simulate either multiple users or high volumes of input data. During execution, response time measurements are taken from selected transaction and these are logged. Performance testing tools normally provide reports based on test logs and graphs of load against response times.	Performance testing specialists
Monitoring tools	Performance and monitoring	Implementation and execution	A software tool or hardware device that runs concurrently with the component or system under test and supervises, records and/or analyses the behaviour of the component or system.	Various
Spreadsheets	Other tools	All activities	Not defined.	Various
SQL	Other tools	Implementation and execution	Not defined.	Various
Project planning/resource	Other tools	Planning and control	Not defined.	Various
Debugging tools	Other tools	Not used for testing activities	A tool used by programmers to reproduce failures, investigate the state of programs and find the corresponding defect. Debuggers enable programmers to execute programs step by step, to halt a program at any program statement and to set and examine program variables.	Developers

INTRODUCING A TOOL INTO AN ORGANIZATION

There are many stages in the process that should be considered before implementing a test tool.

Analyse the problem/opportunity

An assessment should be made of the maturity of the test process used within the organization. If the organization's test processes are immature and ineffective then the most that the tool can do is to make the repetition of these processes quicker and more accurate – quick and accurate ineffective processes are still ineffective!

It is therefore important to identify the strengths, weaknesses and opportunities that exist within the test organization before introducing test tools. Tools should only be implemented that will either support an established test process or support required improvements to an immature test process. It may be beneficial to carry out some TPI (Test Process Improvement) or CMMi (Capability Maturity Model Integration) assessment to establish the maturity of the organization before considering the implementation of any test tool.

Generate alternative solutions

It may be more appropriate and cost effective to do something different. In some organizations, performance testing, which may only need to be done from time to time, could be outsourced to a specialist testing consultancy. Training or recruiting better staff could provide more benefits than implementing a test tool and improve the effectiveness of a test process more significantly. In addition, it is more effective to maintain a manual regression pack so that it accurately reflects the high-risk areas than to automate an outdated regression pack (that is no longer relevant) using a test execution tool.

An early investigation of what tools are available is likely to form part of this activity.

Constraints and requirements

A thorough analysis of the constraints and requirements of the tool should be performed. Interested parties should attend workshops and/or be interviewed.

A formal description of the requirements should be produced and approved by the budget holder and other key stakeholders. A failure to specify accurate requirements (as with a failure to specify accurate requirements for a piece of software) can lead to delays, additional costs and the wrong things being delivered. This could lead to a review process support tool being implemented that does not allow access across the internet, even though there is a need for staff from many countries to participate in reviews.

It is useful to attach some sort of priority or ranking to each requirement or group of requirements.

Training, coaching and mentoring requirements should also be identified. For example, experienced consultants could be used for a few weeks or months to work on overcoming implementation problems with the tool and to help transfer knowledge to permanent staff. Such consultants could be provided by the vendor or could be from the contract market.

Requirements for the tool vendor should also be considered. These could include the quality of training and support offered by the vendor during and after implementation. In addition, the financial stability should be considered as the vendor could go bankrupt. Therefore, using a small niche vendor may be a higher risk than using an established tool supplier.

Evaluation and shortlist

The tools available in the marketplace should be evaluated to identify a short-list of the tools that provide the best fit to the requirements and constraints. This may involve:

- searching the internet;
- attending exhibitions of test tools;
- discussions with tool vendors;
- engaging specialist consultants to identify relevant tools.

It may also be useful for the test organization to send a copy of its list of requirements and constraints to tool vendors so that:

- the vendor is clear about what the test organizations wants;
- the vendor can respond with clarity about what its own tools can do and what workarounds there are to meet the requirements that the tool cannot provide;
- the test organization does not waste time dealing with vendors that cannot satisfy its key requirements.

The outcome of this initial evaluation should result in a shortlist of perhaps one, two or three tools that appear to meet the requirements.

Detailed evaluation/proof of concept

A more detailed evaluation (proof of concept) should then be performed against this shortlist. This should be held at the test organization's premises in the test environment in which the tool will be used. This test environment should use the system under test and other software, operating systems and hardware with which the tool will be used. There are several reasons why there is little benefit from evaluating the tool on something different. For example:

- Test execution tools do not necessarily recognize all object types in the system under test, or they may need to be reconfigured to do so.
- Performance measurement tools may need to be reconfigured to provide meaningful performance information.

- Test management tools may need to have workflow redesigned to support established test processes and may need to be integrated with existing tools used within the test process.
- Static analysis tools may not work on the version of programming languages used.

(Note that if there is only one tool in the shortlist then it may be appropriate to combine the proof of concept and the pilot project.)

After each proof of concept the performance of the tool should be assessed in relation to each predefined requirement. Any additional features demonstrated should be considered and noted as potential future requirements.

Once all proofs of concept have been carried out it may be necessary to amend the requirements as a result of what was found during the tool selection process. Any amendments should be agreed with stakeholders. Each tool should then be assessed against the finalized set of requirements.

There are three likely outcomes at this stage:

- None of the tools meet the requirements sufficiently well to make it worthwhile purchasing and implementing them.
- One tool meets the requirement much better than the others and is likely to be worthwhile. In this case select this tool.
- The situation is unclear and more information is needed. In this case a competitive trial or another cycle/iteration of the process may be needed. Perhaps the requirements need to be revised or further questions need to be put to vendors. It may also be time to start negotiations with vendors about costs.

Negotiations with vendor of selected tool

Once a tool has been selected discussions will be held with the vendor to establish and negotiate the amount of money to be paid and the timing of payments. This will include some or all of the following:

- purchase price
- annual licence fee
- consultancy costs
- training costs
- implementation costs etc.

Discussions should establish the amount to be paid, first, for a pilot project and, secondly (assuming the pilot project is successful), the price to be paid for a larger scale implementation.

The pilot project

The aims of a pilot project include the following:

- It is important to establish what changes need to be made to the high-level processes and practices currently used within the test organization. This involves assessing whether the tool's standard workflow, processes and configuration need to be amended to fit with the test process or whether the existing processes need to be changed to obtain the optimum benefits that the tool can provide.

- To determine lower level detail such as templates, naming standards and other guidelines for using the tool. This can take the form of a user guidelines document.

- To establish whether the tool provides value for money. This is done by trying to estimate and quantify the financial and other benefits of using the tool and then comparing this with the fees paid to the vendor and the projected internal costs to the organization (e.g. lost time that could be used for other things, the cost of hiring contractors, etc.).

- A more intangible aim is to learn more about what the tool can and cannot do and how these functions (or workarounds) can be applied within the test organization to obtain maximum benefit.

The pilot project should report back to the group of stakeholders that determined the requirements of the tool.

If a decision is made to implement the tool on a larger scale then a formal project should be created and managed according to established project management principles. (This is outside the scope of the book and the syllabus. See ISEB Project Management.)

Key factors in successful implementations of test tools

There are certain factors or characteristics that many successful tool implementation projects have in common:

- Implementing findings from the pilot project such as high-level process changes and using functions or workarounds that can add additional benefits.

- Identifying and subsequently writing user guidelines, based on the findings of the pilot project.

- An incremental approach to rolling out the tool into areas where it is likely to be most useful. For example, this can allow 'quick wins' to be made and good publicity obtained, resulting in a generally positive attitude towards the tool.

- Improving the process to fit with the new tool, or amending the use of the tool to fit with existing processes.

- Ensuring that the appropriate level of training, coaching and mentoring is available. Similarly, there may be a need to recruit permanent or contract resources to ensure that sufficient skills exist at the outset of the tool's use within the organization.

- Using a database (in whatever format) of problems encountered and lessons learnt to overcome them. This is because new users are likely to make similar mistakes.

- Capturing metrics to monitor the amount of use of the tool. Recording the benefits obtained. This can then be used to support arguments about implementing to other areas within the test organization.
- Agreeing or obtaining a budget to allow the tool to be implemented appropriately.

Summary of test tool implementation process

The diagram in Figure 6.6 outlines the process for selecting and implementing a test tool in an organization. This shows that there are several points at which a decision could be made **not** to introduce a tool. It also demonstrates that the activities during the evaluation and negotiation stages can follow an iterative process until a decision is made.

CHECK OF UNDERSTANDING

(1) Why is an understanding of the test organization's maturity essential before introducing a test tool?

(2) What is the purpose of defining requirements for the tool?

(3) Why is it important to evaluate the tool vendor as well as the tool itself?

(4) What is meant by a proof of concept?

(5) What is the purpose of a pilot project?

(6) When is it appropriate to combine a proof of concept and pilot project?

(7) Name three factors in the successful implementation of tools.

SUMMARY

We have seen that the main benefits of using test tools are generally the same as the benefits from automating a process in any industry. These are: time saved; and predictable and consistent results.

However, we have also seen that there can be considerable costs in terms of both time and money associated with obtaining such benefits. The point at which the use of tools becomes economically viable depends on the amount of reuse, which is often difficult to predict.

Other risks include over-optimistic expectations of:

- what the tool can do;
- how easy it is to use;
- the amount of maintenance required.

We have seen that there are many types of test tools and that they provide support to a variety of activities within the fundamental test process. We have also seen that tools are used by a variety of staff in the software development process and that some are of greater benefit to developers than testers.

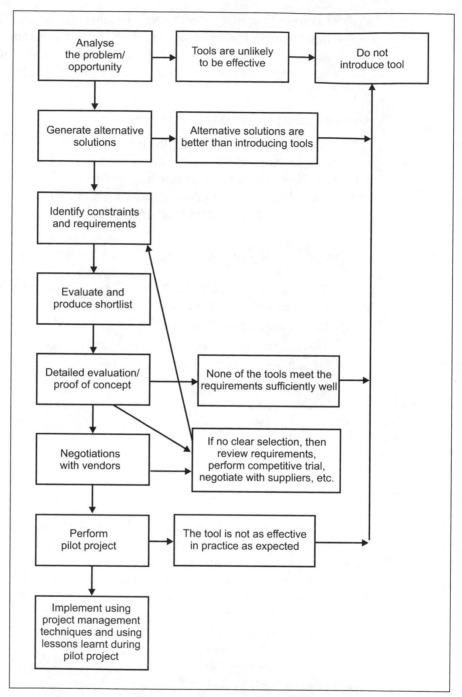

FIGURE 6.6 *Test tool implementation process*

We have looked at the different scripting techniques that can be used with test execution tools. This ranges from the simple record–playback to data-driven and keyword-driven scripts.

We identified a process for selecting and introducing a test tool into an organization. This involves understanding the interactions between activities within the process and examining the purposes of a proof of concept and of a pilot project. We also examined the problems likely to be encountered when implementing a tool and looked at actions that can be taken in an attempt to overcome or avoid such problems.

We also noted that a decision **not** to introduce a tool could well be a valid decision at several stages within the process.

Example Examination Questions with Answers

E1. K1 question

For which of the following activities in the fundamental test process would an incident management tool be **most useful**?

a. Test planning and control
b. Test analysis and design
c. Test implementation and execution
d. Evaluating exit criteria and reporting

E2. K2 question

Which of the following principles should be followed when introducing a test tool into an organization?

(i) Assessing organizational maturity to establish whether a tool will provide expected benefits.
(ii) Requiring a quick payback on the initial investment.
(iii) Including a requirement for the tool to be easy to use without having to train unskilled testers.
(iv) Identifying and agreeing requirements before evaluating test tools.

a. (i) and (ii)
b. (i) and (iv)
c. (ii) and (iii)
d. (iii) and (iv)

E3. K1 question

Which of the following defects is **most likely** to be found by a test harness?

a. Variance from programming standards.
b. A defect in middleware.
c. Memory leaks.
d. Regression defects.

E4. K2 question

How can test execution tools be of **most benefit** during exploratory testing?

a. They can record user actions so that defects are easier to recreate.
b. They can be used to perform the regression aspects of exploratory testing.
c. They can help to mitigate the risk of low test coverage.
d. They can use data-driven tests to increase the amount of exploratory testing performed.

E5. K2 question

Which of the following types of test tool are **most likely** to include traceability functions?

(i)   Performance monitoring tool
(ii) Requirements tool
(iii) Configuration management tool
(iv) Static analysis tool

a.   (i) and (ii)
b.   (i) and (iv)
c.   (ii) and (iii)
d.   (iii) and (iv)

E6. K1 question

A test management tool is **most likely** to integrate with which of the following tools?

a.   Performance management tool
b.   Test data preparation tool
c.   Static analysis tool
d.   Requirements management tool

Answers to questions in the chapter

SA1. The correct answer is d.

SA2. The correct answer is c.

SA3. The correct answer is a.

Answers to example questions

E1. The correct answer is c.

Incident management tools are **most useful** during test implementation and execution as this is the stage at which the tool is used to raise, manage, retest and close incidents.

The data collected during the defect life cycle can then be manipulated into information that is useful for other activities within the fundamental test process.

Information on numbers of defects outstanding may be useful for evaluating exit criteria (option (d)). This information could also be used for planning future testing and for taking control (option (a)).

Incident management tools can also assist in test analysis and design (option (b)) as information about defects found when testing the previous release of the system could be used when analysing the type of testing required for the next enhancement.

E2. The correct answer is b.

Assessing organizational maturity (i) is very important when deciding whether to introduce a test tool, as implementing a tool in an immature test organization with poor processes is unlikely to produce any benefits.

A quick return on the initial investment (ii) in a test tool is rare. See the graph in Figure 6.1.

Having a requirement that a tool should be easy to use for untrained and unskilled testers (iii) is generally a false hope. This is comparable with expecting someone who has never driven a car to be able to drive safely and effectively.

Agreeing requirements before evaluating tools (iv) is essential. Not to do so would be comparable with building and testing a system without requirements.

In conclusion, (i) and (iv) are good principles to follow when introducing a tool and (ii) and (iii) are not.

E3. The correct answer is b.

Variance from programming standards defects (option (a)) are found during the review or static testing process. Therefore a test harness is unlikely to find a defect in programming standards.

Memory leak defects (option (c)) could potentially be found by a test harness designed to run many test cases.

Regression defects (option (d)) could be found using many types of test tool.

Defects in middleware (option (b)) are generally more likely to be found by a test harness or a dynamic analysis tool than by any other type of tool (see Figure 6.5).

E4. The correct answer is a.

Exploratory testing is used when it is unclear what the system is supposed to do. Therefore test execution tools are of little use because expected results cannot be predicted.

However, the record feature of a test execution tool can be used to log the actions performed so that defects can be recreated (option (a)) and rectified more easily.

E5. The correct answer is c.

Requirements management tools (ii) have traceability because they enable test conditions and subsequently test scripts and defects to be traced back to requirements. Configuration management tools (iii) also need to trace the appropriate version of a test script to the release or version of a system or module.

Performance monitoring tools (i) and static analysis tools (iv) are designed for specific objectives. Neither of these tools particularly need traceability functions.

E6. The correct answer is d.

Requirements management tools (option (d)) often have interfaces with test management tools. In some cases they will be sold as a package or in other cases a test management tool may have its own requirements module. The use of such interfaces or integrated packages aids traceability from requirements through to test scripts and defects.

Performance management tools (option (a)), test data preparation tools (option (b)) and static analysis tools (option (c)) are unlikely to have an interface or be integrated with a test management tool. They serve different purposes and therefore there is little need for such interfaces.

7 The Examination

THE EXAMINATION

The examination structure

The Foundation Certificate examination is a one-hour examination made up of 40 multiple choice questions. There are four main aspects to the examination's structure:

- The questions are all equally weighted.
- The number of questions associated with each section of the syllabus is in proportion to the amount of time allocated to that section of the syllabus, which roughly translates into:
  + Section 1, seven questions
  + Section 2, six questions
  + Section 3, three questions
  + Section 4, twelve questions
  + Section 5, eight questions
  + Section 6, four questions

  These proportions are approximate and the precise breakdown is not mandatory, but examinations will be structured along these lines and as close to these relative proportions as possible. In the UK these proportions will be adhered to closely.
- The number of questions at each level of understanding will be as follows:
  + K1 50%, i.e. 20 questions
  + K2 30%, i.e. 12 questions
  + K3 20%, i.e. 8 questions

  This is a mandatory requirement and examinations will adhere more strictly to these proportions than to those related to the syllabus section.

  Since the majority of K3 questions will be likely to be based on Section 4 of the syllabus, it is likely that all or most K3 questions will be about applying test design techniques.
- The pass mark is 25 correct answers and there are no penalties for incorrect answers.

The question types

All questions will contain a 'stem', which states the question and four optional answers. One and only one of the optional answers will be correct. The remainder can be expected to be plausibly incorrect, which means that anyone knowing the correct answer will be unlikely to be drawn to any of the incorrect answers, but anyone unsure of the correct answer will be likely to find one or more alternatives equally plausible.

Questions will be stated as clearly as possible, even emphasizing keywords by emboldening or underlining where this will add clarity. There should be very few negative questions (e.g. which of the following is **not** true?) and any negative questions included will be worded so that there is no ambiguity. Questions will be set to test your knowledge of the content of the topics covered in the syllabus and not your knowledge of the syllabus itself.

There are no absolute rules for question types as long as they are appropriate to the level of understanding they are testing, but there are some common types of questions that are likely to arise.

As a general rule, K1 questions will be of the straightforward variety shown in the next box.

EXAMPLE OF A K1 QUESTION

(This one is taken from Chapter 3.)

What do static analysis tools analyse?
(a) Design
(b) Test cases
(c) Requirements
(d) Program code

K2 questions may be of the same type as the K1 example but with a more searching stem. The more common form of K2 question, however, is known as the Roman type. This is particularly well suited to questions involving comparisons or testing the candidate's ability to identify correct combinations of information. The example in the next box is a K2 question of the Roman type.

EXAMPLE OF A K2 QUESTION

(This example is also from Chapter 3.)

Which of the following statements are correct for walkthroughs?
(i)   Often led by the author.
(ii)   Documented and defined results.
(iii) All participants have defined roles.
(iv)   Used to aid learning.
(v)   Main purpose is to find defects.

(a)   (i) and (v) are correct.

(b)   (ii) and (iii) are correct.

(c)   (i) and (iv) are correct.

(d)   (iii) and (iv) are correct.

K3 questions test the candidate's ability to apply a topic, so the most common form of these is related to test design techniques (though this is not the only topic that can be examined at the K3 level). The next box gives a typical example of a techniques question.

EXAMPLE OF A K3 QUESTION

A system is designed to accept values of examination marks as follows:

Fail	0–39 inclusive
Pass	40–59 inclusive
Merit	60–79 inclusive
Distinction	80–100 inclusive

Which of the following sets of values are all in different equivalence partitions?
(a)   25, 40, 60, 75

(b)   0, 45, 79, 87

(c)   35, 40, 59, 69

(d)   25, 39, 60, 81

Remember that K1, K2 and K3 do not equate to easy, moderate and hard. The K level identifies the level of understanding being tested, not the difficulty of the question. It is perfectly possible to find K2 questions that are more difficult (in the sense of being more challenging to answer) than a K3 question. It is, however, true that K1 questions will always be the most straightforward and anyone who knows the material in the syllabus should have no difficulty in answering any K1 question. Every question has the same value; any 25 correct answers will guarantee a pass.

Remember, too, that topics can be examined at any level up to the maximum identified in the syllabus for that topic, so a K3 topic can be examined at the K1 or the K2 level.

Questions in the examination are not labelled by the K level they are testing, but the example questions at the end of each chapter of this book include examples of K1, K2 and K3 questions, and these are labelled by level for your guidance.

The sample examination

The sample examination paper, which is available from ISEB, is designed to provide guidance on the structure of the paper and the 'rubric' (the rules printed on the front of the paper) of the real examination. The questions in the sample paper are not necessarily typical, though there will be examples of the various types of questions so that candidates are aware of the kinds of questions that can arise. Any topic or type of question in the sample paper can be expected to arise in a real examination at some time. For example, the sample paper may contain an example of a question testing the application of decision testing to a program with a looping structure in it; the existence of this question can be taken to imply that questions involving programs with looping structures may appear in the real examination. Bear in mind that the sample paper may change from time to time to reflect any changes in the syllabus or to reflect any changes in the way questions are set.

Examination technique

In a relatively short examination there is little time to devote to studying the paper in depth. However, it is wise to pause before beginning to answer questions while you assimilate the contents of the question paper. This brief time of inactivity is also a good opportunity to consciously slow down your heart rate and regulate your breathing; nervousness is natural, but it can harm your performance by making you rush. A few minutes spent consciously calming down will be well repaid. There will still be time enough to answer the questions; a strong candidate can answer 40 questions in less than 45 minutes.

When you do start, go through the whole paper answering those questions that are straightforward and for which you know the answer. When you have done this you will have a smaller task to complete and you will probably have taken less than a minute for each question that you have already answered, giving you more time to concentrate on those that you will need more time to answer.

Next, turn to those you feel you understand but that will take you a little time to work out the correct answer, and complete as many of those as you can. The questions you are left with now should be those that you are uncertain about. You now know how long you have to answer each of these and you can take a little more time over each of them.

REVISION TECHNIQUES

There are some golden rules for exam revision:

- Do as many example questions as you can so that you become familiar with the types of questions, the way questions are worded and the levels (K1, K2, K3) of questions that are set in the examination.
- Be active in your reading. This usually means taking notes, but this book has been structured to include regular checks of understanding that will provide you with prompts to ensure you have remembered the key ides from the section you have just revised. In many cases information you need to remember is already in note form for easy learning.
- One important way to engage with the book is to work through all the examples and exercises. If you convince yourself you can do an exercise, but you do not actually attempt it, you will only discover the weakness in that approach when you are sitting in the examination centre.
- Learning and revision need to be reinforced. There are two related ways to do this:
  - ✦ By making structured notes to connect together related ideas. This can be done via lists, but a particularly effective way to make the connections is by using a technique known as mind mapping. An example of a mind map of the syllabus can be found in the Introduction.
  - ✦ By returning to a topic that you have revised to check that you have retained the information. This is best done the day after you first revised the topic and again a week after, if possible. If you begin each revision section by returning to the 'Check of understanding' boxes in some or all of the chapters you worked with in previous revision sessions it will help to ensure that you retain what you are revising.
- Read the syllabus and become familiar with it. Questions are raised directly from the syllabus and often contain wording similar to that used in the syllabus. Familiarity with the syllabus document will more than repay the time you will spend gaining that familiarity.

REVIEW

The layout, structure and style of this book are designed to maximize your learning: by presenting information in a form that is easy to assimilate; by listing things you need to remember; by highlighting key ideas; by providing worked examples; and by providing exercises with solutions. All you need for an intense and effective revision session is in these pages.

The best preparation for any examination is to practise answering as many realistic questions as possible under conditions as close to the real examination as possible. This is one way to use the ISEB sample paper, or you can construct a sample paper of your own from the questions included in this book. Remember to read the syllabus and be sure that you understand what it is asking of you.

Good luck with your Foundation Certificate examination.

Index

1000

700
500
500 — 12 H.
1700
200
300
1200

800
500
500
200
―――
2,000

700 — 200

Bal hal — Rahu
100 600   200
― 300
―――
300
100
―――
400
500
―――
9000

27   27

9
10 2000
    ×10
    ――
    2000
  20000
  2000

LIVERPOOL
JOHN MOORES UNIVERSITY
AVRIL ROBARTS LRC
TITHEBARN STREET
LIVERPOOL L2 2ER
TEL 0151 231 4022